LOVE NEEDS LEARNING

A relationships course for young people

MARGARET VINCENT

GEOFFREY
CHAPMAN

Geoffrey Chapman
A Cassell imprint
Villiers House, 41/47 Strand, London WC2N 5JE
387 Park Avenue South, New York, NY 10016–8810

First edition published by the Catholic Marriage Advisory Council 1989
Second edition first published 1994

Recommended by Rev. Daniel Cavanagh, National Director of the Catholic Marriage Advisory Council of Ireland.

British Library Cataloguing-in-Publication Data
A catalogue record for this book is available from the British Library.

Library of Congress Cataloging-in-Publication Data
Applied for.

ISBN 0–225–66693–6

It may be that some of the ideas and exercises in this book have been adapted by counsellors and others working in relationship education and their original source has been obscured. Every effort has been made to give an acknowledgement wherever possible but should there be any inadvertent errors or omissions, the publishers offer their sincere apologies and will rectify any mistakes in future editions.

Phototypeset by Intype, London
Printed and bound in Great Britain by
Short Run Press Ltd, Exeter

Contents

Foreword

Why on earth does love need learning? On the face of it this seems such an absurd idea in 1993. Television, newspapers, films, songs, magazines and the like seem constantly to be on about love more now than ever before. Mostly, though, it seems to be about beautiful people with beautiful bodies, living in beautiful relationships, in beautiful homes, having beautiful sex.

This can lead people to expect that that is how life ought to be. We can only feel failures against this model. Love seems easy and can be bought or sold. Love, however, is a much used and much misunderstood word, and often confused with sex.

Behind every marriage breakdown and most unsocial behaviour is someone feeling unloved.

The most important element in being able to love and be loved and to live a fulfilling life is a positive self-concept, a reasonable degree of self-esteem.

Sadly, with the increasing rate of breakdown of marriage and family life and the rise in the number of single-parent families, and the enormous economic pressures of living in the 1990s, self-esteem is getting harder to achieve.

Research in 1990 shows that throughout Europe the most important elements in permanent relationships are: mutual respect and appreciation, faithfulness, understanding as well as tolerance, happy sexual relationships.

Similar research conducted in the 1950s shows that at that time the most important requirements were: adequate income, good housing, a good breadwinner and homemaker.

Now we expect our partners to fulfil 100 per cent of our emotional and physical needs. A tall order, yet this can be a really positive sign with potential for deep, fulfilling emotional relationships. Such fulfilment is not easily achieved, as it requires a reasonable degree of self-esteem and an ability to trust and be trusted.

Love has never before needed to be learnt as much as it does now.

Margaret Vincent has had many years' experience as a marriage counsellor, working with individuals and couples with relationship difficulties and in particular with young people, their parents and their teachers. She is therefore the ideal person to produce a resource book to help educators to help young people and indeed anyone to know love and themselves better and to love others.

Margaret has worked with young people in schools, helping them to understand themselves, to learn the skills needed to form and maintain friendships and to explore their values and beliefs, enabling them to develop a thought-through moral code.

Working with parents, she has helped them to understand and listen to their young people and find the best ways of coping with their children's emerging independence and adulthood. She has also been in great demand from teachers to help them to integrate relationship education into the school curriculum. She has a unique understanding of the difficulties faced by teachers as they try and balance their own beliefs, those of the school authorities, and the reality of their pupils' lives.

Anyone who meets Margaret will experience the passionate love and respect that she has for young people. She has great faith in them. As a result they trust and respect her in a way in which the 'older generation' are not usually respected and trusted.

Knowledge alone is not enough. The overweight are the greatest experts in the calorific value of food! Attitudes need to be changed and new skills learned to give people control over their lives and the ability to make choices.

This book, based on Margaret's wide experience, offers a way of developing attitudes, skills and knowledge. Its structure and format demonstrate an understanding of the role of the educator.

The aims of each unit are clearly spelt out and further resources are recommended. The required input is included and the method clearly outlined with a selection of exercises provided. These too include the method, the input, general discussion starters and all necessary handouts.

The contents of this book have been tried and tested by counsellors of the Catholic Marriage Advisory Council and by Margaret Vincent herself. Use it with love to help others to learn to love themselves and others.

Jean Judge
Chief Executive
Catholic Marriage Advisory Council

Introduction

To love is not to give of your riches
but to reveal to others their riches,
their gifts, their value,
and to trust them and their capacity to grow.
So it is important to approach people
in their brokenness and littleness gently
so gently,
not forcing yourself upon them,
but accepting them as they are,
with humility and respect.

Jean Vanier

This book is a revised version of *Love Needs Learning*, originally published by the Catholic Marriage Advisory Council (CMAC). It has grown out of the collective experience of counsellors working not only with estranged couples but also in an educational capacity with engaged couples and adult groups and also with many youth groups in schools, parishes, colleges and universities. The ability to relate well to other people is crucial to our personal development and happiness. Our world is made up of a series of relationships, the quality of which affects dramatically the quality of our lives. The group work designed in this book is intended to help young people understand the skills involved in personal relationships and to encourage them to value friendships that are based on equality and mutual trust. It is concerned with four important areas of growth.

1 POSITIVE SELF-CONCEPT

Research has shown that people who have a positive self-concept have a tremendous advantage in life. They are likely to learn more, achieve more, enjoy more, care more, relate better and generally live more responsible, happy and fulfilled lives.

Self-concept develops from the moment of birth and reflects the degree of love, belongingness and psychological safety we experience. Obviously, the quality of parenting is the most influential factor in the early years. Children who are loved usually grow up respecting themselves and other people. Because they feel psychologically safe they are free to both give and receive love. If, however, our early experiences are unloving, it becomes more difficult to accept ourselves, cope with life and relate well to other people. It is a psychological truth that before we can begin to love other people we have first to learn how to love and accept ourselves, but we cannot do that unless someone has loved us. Love, like deprivation, works in cycles. Nevertheless, although parenting is crucial, as we grow up other factors come into play. The reaction and appraisal of others, peer group acceptance, the comparisons we make of ourselves with others and our ability to succeed, even in small things, will also play a part. All the exercises in this book are concerned with helping young people accept themselves positively and realize their capacity for self-direction and change.

2 SEXUALITY

Many parents find it difficult to talk to their children about sex, invariably because their own education was inadequate, embarrassing or taboo. As sexual people we need to be at ease with our sexuality and acquire positive attitudes towards our bodies. By providing a supportive, non-judgemental atmosphere young people can be encouraged to explore the meaning and responsibilities of sexual behaviour and think through and assess their own sexual values.

3 RELATIONSHIP SKILLS

The ability to relate well is not instinctive. Children learn relationship skills from observing and imitating other people, by experiencing family 'rewards' and 'punishments' and above all by the quality of love they receive. Relationship skills, therefore, vary enormously and many of us acquire inadequate and often destructive ways of communicating with others, e.g. aggression, sulking etc. Relationship skills can, however, be learnt. The experiential work in this book is focused on the acquisition of fundamental communication skills.

4 MORAL DEVELOPMENT

Moral thinking develops with age and depends on intellectual development on the one hand and upon new and challenging experience on the other. (See Piaget and Kohlberg on pp. 6–7 below.)

Young people can be challenged to become more morally aware.

Challenge is an integral part of this programme's exercises, i.e.

> *Self-awareness*
>   leads to
> *Awareness of others*
>   leads to
> *Self-evaluation*
>   leads to
> *Self-discipline*
> as distinct from imposed discipline.

Although this book was intended for use with young people, all the exercises can be adapted for any age group and have been used with groups of teachers, clergy, counsellors etc.

The facilitation of group work needs, however, sensitivity and skill, and group leaders will require some basic training. Nevertheless, the most important qualities required are empathetic listening and a non-judgemental approach.

I would like to thank all the people who have contributed to this book, especially my family and my friends in the CMAC, and in particular Jean Judge for her support, Eileen McCabe for her training and Christopher Robinson for his help and adaptation of the Pinch/Crunch model.

Starting a course
Fundamental considerations

Composition of the group

To build relationships within the group and provide a climate of trust, the size of the group is important. Any number from eight to 14 is viable but less than eight may not provide enough stimulation and more than 14 is unwieldy. Once formed, the group ideally should remain the same and meet regularly.

Atmosphere is important. The group needs to feel comfortable and relaxed. The room needs to be the right size, free from interruptions and warm. Chairs can be arranged in a circle, so that everyone has equal status.

Confidentiality is crucial if members are to trust and value each other. They need to be sure that what is said within the group will not be repeated elsewhere.

Negotiating a contract. It is always helpful to negotiate a contract with members of the group whether they are there voluntarily or not. This means taking time to draw up a list of the group's needs and anxieties.

Work methods for use with small groups

Brainstorming (creative thinking)
Invite members of the group to call out words they immediately associate with a given topic or idea. Everything is accepted and written up without discussion, criticism or judgement. This is essential to encourage as wide-ranging and diverse a list as possible (the more way-out the better).

Role-play
Group members act out a situation, incident or problem in a spontaneous, unrehearsed way. It provides an opportunity for discussion in and out of roles. It is important to de-role each assumed character.

Case studies
Case studies are short descriptions of a real or imagined event that stimulate discussion and require group members to consider decisions, judgements and suggested courses of action.

Games As 'ice-breakers' and to generate interest. Games can be used constructively for many purposes, e.g. to help social inadequacy, to develop sensitivity.

Discussion **Directed discussion.** The group leader manages the group, encourages non-participants and draws attention to different aspects of the subject.

Non-directed discussion. Group leader opens the discussion but withdraws gradually, allowing the group to manage themselves. It gives more practice in interactive social skills than directed discussion.

Buzz groups Small groups (often self-selecting) work on a given idea or issue within a set time-limit, before contributing to the larger group. This helps to create a relaxed atmosphere and more openness in general discussion.

Pairs Group members split into couples and sit facing each other in a relaxed position. For a set period they take it in turns to talk about a given subject, while the other one listens. The listener does not talk or interrupt, only listens. After two minutes they reverse roles.

Triads Pairs are formed and a third person sits at right angles to act as an observer to provide some kind of evaluation of the pair's performance.

Task-centred group A small group (about five people) works on a given task for an allotted time before reporting back to the main group.

Attitude appraisal Appraisal of attitudes on some type of scale.

Open-ended technique A partially stated question or statement to be completed individually, e.g. 'I find it difficult to talk to —'.

Quizzes Individual quizzes usually on different aspects of self, e.g. 'How do I usually express my feelings?'

Outside speakers/videos/ TV/radio Offers expertise and specialist knowledge. Provides a wider perspective.

Handouts To provide basic information.

Reflection A quiet time for reflection, e.g. religious service, meditation, individual quiz, composition, art work etc.

Reference sheet for group leaders

PROFILE OF A HELPFUL GROUP LEADER

- Is well prepared with the objectives and content of the session.
- Has realistic idea of average concentration span, varies activities.
- Good listener.

- Good eye contact and appropriate body language.
- Shows respect for each member of the group.
- Is prepared to stay where the group is, even if it means adapting or redefining the task.
- Demonstrates empathy, i.e. understanding of how members of the group are feeling.
- Able to challenge constructively.
- Non-judgemental.
- Non-didactic.
- Uses appropriate language to convey meaning.
- Asks open-ended questions, e.g. 'How?' 'What do you think?'
- Acts as a facilitator.
- Encourages concreteness, e.g. 'Can you give an example?'
- Summarizes at intervals and checks out what is being said, e.g. 'Right, what you are saying is —'.
- Notices and comments on any disparity between verbal and non-verbal messages.
- Reflects back what is being said and provides clarification if necessary.

PROFILE OF AN UNHELPFUL GROUP LEADER

- Inflexible and unimaginative.
- Bad time-keeper.
- Not prepared for the session.
- Judgemental.
- Shows boredom, impatience or condescension.
- Didactic.
- Talks too much.
- Asks too many closed questions.
- Does not value contributions equally.
- Allows strong members of the group to dominate the discussion.
- Uses inappropriate language.
- Imposes own opinions, perceptions or beliefs.
- Is uncomfortable with silence and rushes in too quickly.
- Interrupts.

Group leader initiatives

QUESTIONS THAT HELP TO STIMULATE GROUP DISCUSSION

- How easy/difficult did you find that?
- Why?
- How did you feel about coming today?
- How did that feel?
- What was it like when I asked you to do that?
- Could you give an example?
- Could you expand that a little more?
- Could you give more details?
- Can you see any connection between this and that?
- What does the word (e.g. love, respect) mean to you?

- What do you think?
- What do you like/dislike about . . .?

RESPONSES TO A DIFFICULT GROUP

- What are you finding difficult about the session?
- I sense you are not finding the work we are doing very helpful. Would you like to say anything about it?
- Does anyone agree with that?
- What do you think?
- I don't see it that way myself. Would anyone else like to comment on that?
- Perhaps we could take the opportunity to discuss this later?
- Sorry, I didn't explain myself clearly.
- That's an interesting point of view. How do the rest of you feel?
- Did anyone get anything out of it?
- Tell us more about . . .
- What do you think the consequences of adopting this point of view would be?
- Perhaps there are other points of view. Can you think of any?

STAGES OF DEVELOPMENT IN GROUPS
(Based on B. W. Tuckman's Theory of Group Development)

It is helpful for the group leader to understand that groups mature and develop and have four recognizable stages (five if *endings* are included). Awareness of these stages can be reassuring, particularly the knowledge that *storming* is a normal and creative stage of the group's development.

1 Forming   The group is not yet a group but a set of individuals. Group members may:

Try to define their own roles	Be dependent on leader
Suspect the task	Avoid the real work
Exchange information	Suspect other people
Get involved	Organize other people
	Withdraw

2 Storming   Most groups go through a conflict stage. Group members may:

Question the value of their role	Challenge the leader
Challenge the work and methods	Display hostility
Take sides, pacify, defend, attack	Become very active or passive

3 Norming   The group starts to establish how the group will perform, e.g. when and how to work, the degree of trust, openness, confidence that are going to be appropriate. Group members may:

Begin to open up and self-disclose

Express feelings constructively

Redefine the task

Support suggestions from others

Invite others' opinions

Support the leader

Clarify

4 Performing The group reaches a stage of constructive performing. Group members may:

Work energetically to achieve results

Collaborate effectively

Become committed to success

Focus on task

Contribute

Feel part of the group

What the experts say about adolescence and early adulthood

FREUD

The genital stage. The libido (sexual energy) is directed towards heterosexual pleasure.

ALLPORT PERSONALITY MODEL

According to the American psychologist Gordon W. Allport, personality traits, previously disparate and inconsistent, become integrated into a single mature personality. Inconsistent behaviour in adolescence is normal in striving towards maturity. Maturity is recognizable by certain characteristics:

Empathy — the ability to identify with others, i.e. an extended sense of self; the ability to relate to others in a warm, unselfish manner.

Self-awareness — realistic view and acceptance of self.

A realistic orientation towards the world.

A consistent, coherent view of the purpose of life, i.e. a unifying philosophy that determines values and life goals.

ERIKSON'S IDENTITY THEORY
(E. H. Erikson, *Childhood and Society* (1962))

The emergence of more mature life goals. There is a transition from the fluid personality of the child (Allport's traits and selves) to the more constant one of the adult. The task for the adolescent is to achieve an adult identity described as 'a feeling of being at home in one's body, a sense of knowing where one is going and an inner assuredness of anticipated recognition from those who count'. This involves experimenting, trying out roles before adopting them permanently. Adolescents turn to their peer group for support and model themselves on the people they admire. It becomes increasingly important to be accepted as sexually attractive, although Elkind suggests that:

At this stage falling in love is not entirely, or even primarily, a sexual matter . . . but an attempt to arrive at a definition of one's identity by projecting one's diffused self-image on another, seeing it thus reflected and gradually clarified. This to my mind is why so much young love is conversation.

(D. Elkind, *Children and Adolescents: Interpretive Essays on Jean Piaget* (New York: OUP, 1974))

Theories of development: cognitive and moral

PIAGET

The onset of adolescence sees the emergence of 'formal operations', an advanced level of thinking, i.e. hypothetical–deductive reasoning, the ability to reason abstractly about a hypothetical problem. It is now agreed that not all reach the most advanced level of formal thought.

ELKIND

Elkind has extended our notion of adolescent reasoning with the notion of adolescent egocentrism. The achievement of formal operational thought enables the adolescent to take into account not only his or her own thought but the thought of other people. The problem is that they find it difficult to differentiate between what others are thinking and their own preoccupations, e.g. personal appearance. Elkind describes this egocentrism in terms of an 'imaginary audience' and believes that a lot of teenage behaviour — self-consciousness, long hours in front of the mirror, and a need for privacy — can be explained in terms of the heightened awareness at this age of the reactions of others in actual or fantasized social situations. Another concept introduced by Elkind is the 'personal fable'. Because of the adolescent's preoccupation with an 'imaginary audience' a 'personal fable' emerges which is, in essence, the individual's story about themselves, which will probably include fantasies of omnipotence and immortality.

PIAGET AND KOHLBERG

The Swiss psychologist Jean Piaget (1896–1980) originated the cognitive and developmental approach to moral thinking later elaborated by the American Lawrence Kohlberg (b. 1927). This approach argues that the way children reason about moral issues changes in a systemic fashion with age. Kohlberg's theory sees the child passing through six major stages in moral development. With the acquisition of formal operational thinking the later stages of moral thinking can be achieved. Pre-conventional and conventional morality are superseded by post-conventional morality, where rules are increasingly seen as arbitrary and subject to possible and sometimes desirable change. At this stage moral ideas become integrated into a consistent philosophy. Moral development, as seen by Kohlberg, relies greatly on the ability to imagine what it feels like to be someone else, actually to experience the same feelings, i.e. to empathize. As adolescents develop a consistent philosophy and clarify their own values, their moral behaviour should become self-sustaining, but at the earlier stages they need boundaries, good models and reinforcement of good behaviour. Like cognitive development, adolescents will develop at different rates and some will not achieve the later stages.

HAVIGHURST: THE DEVELOPMENTAL TASKS OF ADOLESCENCE

Robert J. Havighurst sees adolescence in terms of the achievement of developmental tasks:

1   Achieving new and mature relationships with peer group friends of both sexes.

2   Achieving a female and male social role.

3   Accepting one's physique and using the body effectively.

4   Achieving emotional independence of parents and adults.

5   Preparing for marriage, long-term relationships and family life.

6   Preparing for an economic career.

7   Acquiring a set of values and an ethical system as a guide to behaviour.

Who am I?

AIMS The group will:

1 Look at the way they see themselves and test their perceptions against the way other people see them.

2 Examine some of the influences in their lives.

3 Recognize the connection between a positive self-esteem and the ability to relate well to other people.

4 Make a rough appraisal of their own self-esteem and see ways of improving it.

5 Appreciate the effect their behaviour can have on other people's self-esteem.

Who am I?

INPUT Adolescence is an age-related transition that happens to all of us. It is the transition from childhood to adulthood and like all changes it involves some loss. A transition is the time of uncertainty that occurs between moving from one, more or less familiar, way of life, to another new and unfamiliar one. It is a time of confusion when new patterns of behaviour have slowly to be established. It is a time of questioning, experimenting and changing relationships, when self-esteem is particularly fragile.

The big question that teenagers have to struggle with is 'Who am I?' Their developmental task is to achieve a sense of identity described as 'a feeling of being at home in one's body, a sense of knowing where one is going and an inner assuredness of anticipated recognition from those who count' (Elkind).

Penalties for not doing so result in numerous problems, e.g. identity confusion, drugs, alcohol, premature intimacy and the formation of a negative identity. Adolescence is a stressful time for any youngster, but particularly so for those whose self-esteem is already low. Other people can wittingly or unwittingly contribute to it, thus reinforcing their feelings of inadequacy and hopelessness. As they are encouraged to explore who they are, what they hope for in their relationships, and what they have to offer to other people, it is important that they do so in a supportive atmosphere. Constructive responses, empathetic listening and respect are required if they are to be enabled to accept a more positive attitude towards themselves.

Ice breaker

Everyone in the group introduces themselves by their first name and an adjective that begins with the same initial as their first name, e.g. magnificent Mary, interesting Indira, talkative Tom, etc.

Exercise 1 — IF I WERE . . .

Individually complete one of the following sentences:

If I were a flower I would be _____
If I were an animal I would be _____
If I were a colour I would be _____
If I were a car I would be _____

Small groups

Take it in turns to share your image of yourself as a flower, animal etc. Explain why you chose it. Then invite the other people in the group to choose another image that they think suits you. Does it fit in with your own image of yourself? Ask them to explain the reasons for their choice and be prepared to disagree with anything you don't like (e.g. if you saw yourself as a rose you would probably be surprised if someone else saw you as a red hot poker!). Give concrete reasons why you don't want to accept their image of you. Only accept images you like.

General discussion

What did you learn about yourselves?

Exercise 2 — GROUP CONTRACT: WHERE DO WE GO FROM HERE?

Method

Group members (NB: this includes the group leader) write down their answers to the following questions:

1   What do you hope to get out of this group work?

2   What are you afraid you might get, i.e. what don't you want?

3   What could you or other members of the group do to stop you getting what you want?

Into pairs

Couples share their answers with each other and try to add to them. Allow ten minutes.

Main group

Group leader invites people to call out their *hopes* and *fears* and lists them on a large sheet of paper that is then displayed on the wall for future reference. The group is then aware of all the things that could sabotage their work together. From these they can draw up their own set of group rules, e.g.

Sample group contract
Every member of our group agrees:

1   What is said in the group is private to the group.

2   Everyone's contribution is of equal value.

3   When someone is talking the others listen.

4   No put-downs or rubbishing other people.

5   No smoking.

6   No whispering or private conversations.

Exercise 3   MIRROR IMAGE

See p. 52.

Exercise 4   GET TO KNOW ME

Preparation   The group facilitator needs to prepare beforehand for this exercise. Each of the sentences on p. 53 has to be copied on to a small piece of cardboard and placed in some kind of container, e.g. a hat, waste-paper basket etc.

Method   This exercise is most effective in small groups (eight to twelve). Each member of the group, in turn, draws one item from the container and completes the sentence out loud. Anyone has the right to pass, in which case the uncompleted sentence is offered to the group and any member can offer to complete it. If no one volunteers it should be put to one side until the end of the exercise. Continue round the group until the container is empty.

General discussion   How easy/difficult did you find it to give your own ideas in public? Why do you think you found it easy/difficult?

How can you become more confident about yourselves?

How do you benefit from listening to other people's contributions?

What can you do to help somebody else become more confident about themselves? List the helps.

What can you do to prevent someone else becoming more confident about themselves? Why might you want to hinder someone rather than help them?

Were there any questions that nobody wanted to answer? If yes, what was it that made these questions difficult to answer?

Exercise 5   PIGGY IN THE MIDDLE

Into pairs   Partners tell each other which position they come in their family. Are they the oldest, in the middle, or the youngest? What is it like to be in that position?

General discussion

What are the advantages/disadvantages of being the oldest in the family?

What are the advantages/disadvantages of being in the middle?

What are the advantages/disadvantages of being the youngest?

If you could have chosen, where would you have liked to come in the family? Why?

Exercise 6   MY HERO

Method

Individually, each person in the group writes down the names of the three people (male or female, fact or fiction) they most admire. Into Buzz groups to share their choices and the reasons for their choice. With the help of the Buzz group each person has to decide which two of their three choices they will now eliminate, so that they are left with only one hero. (Allow 15 minutes.)

Main group

Each member of the group writes up their chosen hero on the flip-chart. The task for the group is then to choose from the list *one* hero only to represent the group as a whole. The choice should be democratic, with members of the group arguing the merits of their own choice and pointing out the defects of others. Unless the decision is unanimous, a show of hands will elect the winner.

Once the hero has been chosen the group can discuss the following issues:

What was it about the group hero that made her/him the winner?

What values do you think your group hero embodies?

Are you happy with these values? If yes, why? If no, why not?

Do the people we admire influence our lives or behaviour in any way?

Personal reflection

Write down on a piece of paper the names of the three heroes you originally chose, and list all the qualities you admire in them. What, if anything, does it tell you about yourself?

Exercise 7   FEELING GOOD

Brainstorm

What makes us feel good?

Sample brainstorm

Praise	Good news	Treat	Surprises
Compliments	Kisses	Presents	Popularity
Success	New clothes	Chocolate	Doing
Admiration	Making others	Hugs	something well
Being right	happy	Laughs	Friends
Being wanted	Being loved	Courtesy	

Into pairs	Think of some event or somebody who has made you feel good during the past week (extend to a month if necessary). Describe what happened and what it felt like.

General discussion	Everybody likes to feel good about themselves, but how good are you at helping other people feel good?

How good are you at making yourselves feel good? How much of your 'self-talk', i.e. the conversations you have with yourselves inside your heads, is positive or negative? ('Nobody likes me — I'm boring', 'I can't do it', or 'I can't expect the whole world to like me. Too bad', 'I can do the best I can'.)

Is it difficult to say the things you like about yourself? Try it out by going around the group and asking each member to say two things they like about themselves.

Would it have been easier to say two things you disliked about yourselves? If so, why?

Is there any connection between the way you feel about yourselves and the way you respond to other people?

Why, do you think, is it important that you learn to change the tape within your heads from negative to positive?

(The concept of positive and negative tapes comes from the theory of Transactional Analysis.)

Exercise 8   HOW DO I SEE MYSELF?

See p. 54.

Exercise 9   INSTANT GLOW

Each person will need a long blank piece of paper and a pen or pencil.

Method	Each member of the group writes their name at the bottom of the piece of paper, then bends it over so that their name is facing outwards. They pass it to the person on their left-hand side who then writes at the top of the paper one good thing about the person whose name is written at the bottom. It must be positive and unqualified, i.e. no 'ifs' or 'buts'. The writer then folds the paper to hide what is written and passes it to the next person on the left. The exercise is repeated until each person in the group gets their own paper back. Then everyone together opens their praise lists just like Christmas presents.

Group discussion	How did you feel about your praise lists?

Was anyone surprised by what was written about them? Can they accept it?

How difficult is it to praise other people genuinely?

Do you think there is any connection between the way we feel about ourselves and the way we see other people?

Research has shown that the more able we are to give genuine praise to others (praise that is not genuine is in fact experienced as the opposite, i.e. a put-down), the more we get ourselves. How many people have you complimented, praised or in some way made feel good in the past week? How many people have complimented, praised or made you feel good in the past week? Any connection?

Exercise 10   REFLECTIVE EXERCISE

See p. 55.

Recommended resources   Donna Brandes and Howard Phillips, **Gamesters Handbook 1 and 2** (Lifeskills Associates).

Barrie Hopson and Mike Scally, **Life Skills Programme No. 1** (Lifeskills Associates).

Kate Eunson and Michael Henderson, **Coping with Shyness and Loneliness** (Chambers, 1987).

How about you?

AIMS The group will:

1 **Examine some of their own attitudes towards other people for signs of bias and prejudice.**
2 **Be encouraged to express their feelings and reactions to the way they are stereotyped by other people.**
3 **Reflect upon the effect their behaviour has on other people.**

Who are you?

INPUT The ability to relate well to other people is crucial. It is only through rewarding relationships that we learn to fulfil our own potential and achieve personal happiness. It is only through interactions with other people that we become fully human and fully alive. Getting along with all the people in our lives is not easy but it is vitally important. We rely on others for warmth, stimulation, affection and love. It used to be thought that the ability to relate was instinctive but we now know that it is also learnt. Relationship skills depend on a positive self-concept and honest communication, and are summed up in three words — respect, empathy and genuineness. The more people we relate well to, the more we learn about ourselves and humanity.

Unfortunately, however, we often dismiss people through unjust and distorting 'stereotyping'. Instead of being open to people we block them out by categorizing them by external features, e.g. age, gender, appearance, dress, race, class, sexual orientation etc. It enables us to make assumptions about individuals without any real knowledge of them. We distance ourselves from them so that no respect, empathy, or genuineness is possible. Labels create a 'them' and 'us' mentality which invariably leads to prejudice and discrimination. The word 'stereotype' originates from the Greek *stereos* meaning 'solid' and *typos* meaning 'image': solid image. Our stereotypes can be either negative or positive. Negative stereotyping caricatures critically, e.g. all old people are ga-ga. Positive stereotyping is blinded by illusion, e.g. French men are great lovers.

Of course, when we first meet people we classify them in some way or other, but whatever short cuts we take we need to revise our first impressions in the light of our actual experience of the individual, and not make judgements on mere inferences or prejudices.

The task of this unit is to help the group examine their attitudes towards other people for prejudice and stereotyping and to recognize illusions and idealizations as part of the process. We have to accept people as they are, not as we think they are, if we are going to develop mature relationships.

Exercise 11   HELPS AND HINDRANCES

Method   Split into two groups. One group brainstorms what makes relationships work while the other group looks at what hinders relationships. Both groups list their 'Helps' and 'Hindrances' on large sheets of paper. After ten minutes reassemble into one group. Before pinning the sheets on the wall, see if anyone wishes to add anything extra to either of the lists. Display sheets where they can be seen by everyone.

Input   Research has shown that there is a 'holy trinity' of relationship skills. They are:

REG	or put another way	**RUBY**
Respect		Respect
Empathy		Understanding
Genuineness		Be
		Yourself

Reg and Ruby: the ideal couple

(Originally devised by Leeds Counselling and Career Unit, University of Leeds)

General discussion   How do you show respect towards other people? How many of the Helps on the list come under the heading of respect? Underline them with a coloured marker.

How do you show empathy towards other people? How many of the Helps on the list come under the heading of empathy? Underline with a second coloured marker.

How do you demonstrate genuineness towards other people? How many of the Helps on the list come under the heading of genuineness?

Looking at your list of Hindrances which of them show (a) lack of respect? (b) lack of empathy? (c) lack of genuineness?

Into pairs   Think of one person you are finding it difficult to get along with at the moment. Try to tell your partner why you think you are having trouble relating to this particular person, and why you think they are having trouble relating to you. After eight minutes change over so that the speaker becomes the listener.

Exercise 12   WHAT'S IN A FACE?

Method   Divide into small groups (six to eight). Pass the four pictures or photographs around the group (see sheet on p. 56).

Allow ten minutes discussion time and then ask each group to try and reach a unanimous decision before returning to the main group.

(NB: This exercise is easily adapted by choosing different pictures and providing a new story-line. Newspapers and magazines provide a rich source of material. The pictures should show two people or pairs of people of roughly the same age who project different images of themselves by their physical type, facial expressions, haircuts, clothes etc. The story-line should be simple, e.g. your school is appointing a new PE teacher — who would you prefer to get the job?)

General discussion

Was it a unanimous decision, or did anyone disagree?

Were any personal qualities attributed to the photographs, e.g. kind, warm, stern, mean, fun, thoughtful?

How much do you really know about these four people?

Although this is an artificial exercise, because you were expected to make a choice out of four photographs, how much do you think we judge people by their external appearance?

Are physical characteristics a good guide to (a) personality, (b) character?

Exercise 13

LABELS

Method

Group leader writes on the flipchart all the labels she/he imagines other people might use to describe her/him, e.g.

Sample labels for group leader

Female	Lapsed Catholic
Intellectual	Middle-aged
Working class	Mother
Do-gooder	Widow
Feminist	Aggressive

Into pairs

Partners help each other to think of all the labels that other people might apply to them. Then each chooses the label they hate most. They write this on a label and stick or pin it on their chests. (Allow ten minutes.)

Walk around the room looking at everybody else's labels. If someone has the same label join up with them and talk about what it feels like to be labelled ___. Any others that are left with an 'odd man out' label join together and talk about what it feels like to have a distinctive label.

General discussion

How many chose the same label?

If you found that others had chosen the same label (a) how did it feel? (b) did it help?

How does it feel if no one else had the same label?

When we label people we infer or guess things about their personality and character. Do we also guess about the way they will behave? How reliable do you think these guesses are?

(a) How often do we label people? (b) Having labelled them, how often do we dismiss them as not worth knowing?

Why do you think we label people in this way?

Exercise 14

ALL IN THE NAME (ATTITUDE CONTINUUM)

Method

Group leader draws an imaginary line down the middle of the room and stands on a chair in the middle of it. He/she then reads out the statements below, one at a time, and invites members of the group to place themselves along the line according to whether they agree or disagree with the statement. The extreme right-hand side of the line represents complete agreement with the statement, the extreme left-hand side of the line represents disagreement with the statement. In the middle represents the 'don't knows'. How strongly people feel can be shown by where they stand along the line.

Attitude statements

Large families are happy families.

The homeless prefer to live on the streets and beg rather than work.

Accountants are boring.

All politicians are dishonest.

Women are illogical.

Teachers teach because they can't do anything else.

The Irish are thick.

Immigrants only come to this country to live off the State.

Adolescents are rowdy and ill-mannered.

Nurses are compassionate and dedicated.

Catholics are very superstitious.

General discussion

All the statements were based on stereotypes. How many statements did you agree with? How prejudiced were we as a group?

Where do these attitudes based on stereotypes come from? How do we acquire them?

Is there any element of truth in stereotypes?

We can stereotype both negatively and positively (statements 1 and 10). Is one less distorting than the other? If yes, why is this so? If no, why not? What do the two types of stereotyping have in common?

Are there occasions when stereotyping can be dangerous?

Exercise 15

CASE STUDY: MARIKA

See p. 57.

Exercise 16   ROLE-PLAY

Method   Divide into small groups (four to six). Ask each group to decide the label they would least like to have applied to them, e.g. dyke, Jew-boy, Superwoman etc. and create a role-play around it. Players should ad lib and develop the parts in their own way from a basic story-line. (Allow 15 to 20 minutes.) Each group then takes it in turn to role-play in front of the others, who provide the audience. *Remember to de-role the players at the end of each role-play.*

There should be a general discussion involving everybody at the end of each role-play, covering the following points:

How did each player feel in their character part?

Were others surprised at the way they felt?

What was the outcome of the role-play? Was it realistic?

Was there a more satisfactory way of dealing with the situation?

What is the best way to deal with prejudice?

Exercise 17   DOWNERS

Input   Being labelled can make us feel lonely and isolated. What other things, do you think, give us a downer?

Brainstorm   What makes us feel bad about ourselves?

Sample brainstorm

Failure	Criticism	Spots
Rejection	Sarcasm	Rows
Guilt	Being left out	Appearance
Being fat	Being skinny	Anxiety
Undervalued	Neglected	Hurt
Undermined	Mocked	Unloved

General discussion   A 'put-down' is when someone makes us feel small or humiliated. Can you remember a time when you were put down and share it with the group? (Group leader starts off with own experience and then invites other members to contribute their own examples of put-downs.)

How does it feel to be put down?

Do you ever put yourself down? How? Why?

Are you in any way responsible for the way others see you?

How do you feel when you put other people down? Does it give you a buzz or a downer?

Are you in any way responsible for the way other people see themselves?

How can you avoid put-downs in this group?

Exercise 18	**CASE STUDY: JENNY**

See p. 58.

Exercise 19	**REFLECTIVE EXERCISE**

See p. 59.

Recommended resources

Barrie Hopson and Mike Scally, **Life Skills Programme No. 1** (Lifeskills Associates).

Barrie Hopson and Mike Scally, **Life Skills Programme No. 2** (Lifeskills Associates).

Richard Nelson-Jones, **Human Relationship Skills**, 2nd edition (Cassell, 1990).

How well do I communicate with you?

AIMS **The group will:**

1 **Review their own skills in communication.**

2 **Practise and interpret body language and learn to become sensitive to its meaning.**

3 **Identify barriers to communication.**

4 **Begin to acquire the skill of empathetic listening.**

How well do I communicate with you?

INPUT Communication is instinctive. We have to communicate to survive. A baby's first cry demands attention and initiates an immediate and continuous interaction with the parent or substitute parent. Communication is, however, also learnt. Children learn their skills from observing and imitating other people (family and other models), from their own experience of rewarding and punishing behaviour and, above all, by the quality of the love they receive.

The ability to communicate varies enormously. We grow up in different families with different life-styles and different ways of communicating with each other. Some are effective, others are not. Many people acquire inadequate and sometimes destructive ways of communicating with each other, e.g. shouting, sulking, criticizing etc. Instead of becoming closer and more intimate in their relationships they erect barriers and can easily become more and more detached and isolated from other people. Messages become distorted and interpretations inaccurate.

Our lives are full of people with whom we communicate in different ways and with different degrees of closeness, e.g. acquaintances, friends, family etc. (Try jotting down the names of everybody you have spoken to today. How well do you know them? How does that affect the way you communicate with them?)

John Powell sj in his book *Why Am I Afraid to Tell You Who I Am?* suggests that we use five different levels of communicating with other people, depending on how close we are to them. The more we can share of ourselves, the closer we can become.

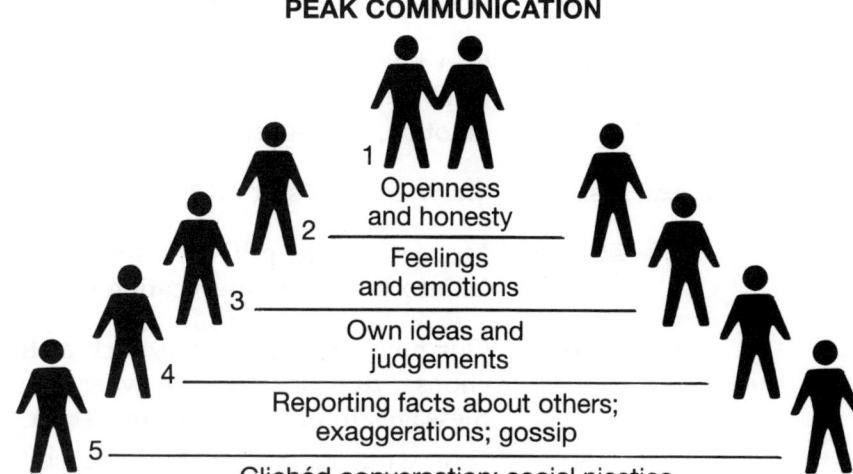

PEAK COMMUNICATION

1 — Openness and honesty

2 — Feelings and emotions

3 — Own ideas and judgements

4 — Reporting facts about others; exaggerations; gossip

5 — Clichéd conversation; social niceties

To be honest and open about ourselves, however, is always risky. We make ourselves vulnerable to hurt and rejection — but we also open ourselves to intimacy and love and friendship. Good communication needs to be appropriate but invariably depends on clear messages about who I am, what I need, what I feel, fear and value. This involves accepting personal responsibility for our feelings and actions. It involves looking at ourselves clearly and valuing what we see.

Human communication

Human beings, unlike animals, have two channels of communication: verbal and non-verbal.

VERBAL COMMUNICATION

has a grammatical structure and conveys information about events outside itself. It is used primarily for conveying information.

NON-VERBAL COMMUNICATION

is used for communicating interpersonal attitudes and emotions, supporting verbal communication, and in some situations replacing speech. The most influential work on non-verbal communication is Charles Darwin's *The Expression of Emotions in Man and Animals*.

NON-VERBAL SIGNALS

Body contact Shows friendship and degree of intimacy, used in greetings and farewells.

Body proximity There are cross-cultural differences in what is accepted as comfortable body distance between people. Arabs, for example, stand closer together than the British. People sit or stand closer to those they know and like. If a stranger or an acquaintance comes too close, feelings of discomfort and embarrassment result in further distancing.

Body orientation	The way we point our body indicates co-operation, competition, hostility, liking etc.
Body posture	Body posture mirrors tension, tiredness, confidence, relaxation etc.
Gestures	Can reinforce what we are saying or complete our meaning. They can be used on their own, as in sign language, or to show a particular emotion, e.g. aggression.
Facial expressions	Show emotions or attitudes.
Eye signals	Movements, length and direction of gaze are very important for 'comfortable' communication between people.
Appearance	Our physical appearance, such as the way we dress, the colours we choose, the make-up we wear, our current hair-style, will convey messages to others about our status, occupation and personality.

(Adapted from The Open University, D305, Block 11, Social Psychology.)

Exercise 20 — HOW DO WE COMMUNICATE?

Brainstorm

How do people communicate with each other?

Sample brainstorm

Talking	TV	Opera
Shaking hands	Telephone	Swearing
Kissing	Smoke-signals	Dancing
Gestures	Sex	Gifts
Touching	Poetry	Morse code
Drama	Sport	Flags
Music	Religion	Shouting
Listening	Symbols	Sign language
Appearance	Tone of voice	Crying
Thought-waves	Pigeon post	Grimacing
Art	Tapes	Thumping
Radio	Rape	

At the end of the brainstorm the group can discuss which items on the list are verbal and which are non-verbal. It is helpful to underline the non-verbals to highlight their significance. If not mentioned, 'Listening' needs to be added and underlined in a different coloured pen to make it stand out.

Group discussion

Which is more important: what we say or the way we say it?

Exercise 21 — WHAT YOU SAY AND WHAT YOU MEAN ARE TWO DIFFERENT THINGS

Method 1

Group leader asks members of the group to demonstrate, without speaking or moving from their chairs, the following emotions:

Anger	Misery
Nervousness	Excitement
Boredom	Interest
Happiness	Shock

How easy or difficult was it for the rest of the group to recognize the emotion?

Method 2 This is a silent-movie session. Show a video of any popular programme without the soundtrack for ten minutes. The group's task is to note as many non-verbal signals as possible. How much of the story-line were they able to follow? Research suggests that 65 per cent of conversation is non-verbal. Does the 'silent movie' bear this finding out or not?

Method 3 The group leader models 'out of synch' communication. A message is given to the group demonstrating conflicting verbal and non-verbal messages, e.g. arms folded tightly across the chest while saying 'How lovely to see you'.

Divide the group into pairs and give them five minutes to try out conflicting messages for themselves.

Also in pairs, one person attempts to talk to their partner whose task it is to try, through their non-verbal behaviour only, to shut them up!

General discussion In the group as a whole, discuss:

What kinds of non-verbal behaviour people used to try and stop their partner speaking. (*List them.*)

How easy or difficult did they find it to continue talking when their partner displayed a lack of interest in what they were saying?

How did it feel to be (a) the speaker (b) the listener?

If, as research has shown, non-verbal signals are five times as strong as verbal ones, what implications does this have for our day-to-day communication with other people?

Listening

Input Good listeners are rarely lonely. Listening is an underrated skill but good listeners attract other people to them. 'I can really talk to her', 'Sam is great! He always seems to understand how I feel.'

Because life is pressurized ordinary listening activity tends to be automatic. Stimuli crowd in on us from all directions, so the brain filters out the vital components we need to hear and suppresses the rest. A good example of this is the 'cocktail party syndrome' where, above all the hubbub of party talk, if your own name is mentioned the ear will pick it up, even if it is spoken quite softly. (You might like to test this out with the group.)

Often, and not unnaturally, we are dashing around, preoccupied with the routine tasks of life and so anxious to communicate our own ideas and opinions that we forget other people and have no interest in listening to them. 'Well, I think...', 'Sorry, I must dash...'.

Yet, if we are to get to know people, make friends and relate successfully 'active listening' is essential. Active listening is really listening with empathy. Empathy has been described as 'the ability to identify with somebody else, to think as they think, feel as they feel, to enter temporarily their inner world'. Less grandiosely, it is the ability to put yourself in someone's shoes and imagine what it feels like to be them. It is a skill that seems to come naturally to a few people, but it can be learnt through practice and experience. The following exercises may seem artificial and difficult because they cut across normal behaviour, but they provide a model of active listening and encourage awareness and improvement of individual and group listening skills.

Exercise 22   HOW DID THAT FEEL?

Method

Split into pairs. Couples sit facing each other. Group leader designates each person as an A or B and instructs them to start a normal conversation. After two minutes of talking the group leader announces that instructions are going to be called out at two-minute intervals which they are to follow, while at the same time continuing to talk to each other.

'Keep talking' is the golden rule.

The following instructions are then read out at two-minute intervals.

A remains sitting.	B stands.
A stands.	B sits down.
A remains standing.	B stands.
A closes eyes.	B keeps eyes open.
A opens eyes.	B closes eyes.
A closes eyes.	B keeps eyes closed.
A opens eyes.	B opens eyes and turns back on A.
A turns back on B.	B keeps back turned to A.
A sits down.	B sits down.

General discussion   How did that feel?

Exercise 23   SOLER RULES OK!

Sit opposite
Open position
Lean forward
Eye contact
Relax

Method Divide into chosen pairs and sit squarely facing each other. Each couple take it in turns to be (a) the speaker (b) the listener. The listener should show by the way they sit that they are attentive to what is being said. This means following the SOLER rules, i.e. sitting in an open position directly opposite the speaker, not crossing arms or legs, maintaining good eye contact and leaning slightly towards the speaker to show involvement.

The speaker then has two minutes to talk about 'The best/worst thing that has happened to me this week'. The listener's task is to listen not only to the words but the feelings behind the words. This means listening to the words *without interruption* and empathizing with the speaker's feelings. Their response should reflect back these feelings to the speaker, i.e. 'You feel ____ because ____'.

(NB: It doesn't matter if the listener is not completely accurate in identifying the feelings. By reflecting back their observations they offer the speaker the opportunity to correct and clarify for themselves what they experienced, e.g. 'Well, it wasn't anger as much as disappointment. I felt really sad.')

After two minutes reverse the roles and repeat the exercise.

The group leader will need to check out each couple to see:

How well did the listener listen?

Which was easier, to talk or to listen?

How did the listener encourage the speaker to keep on talking?

How important were gestures, facial expressions etc.?

A good listener will mirror the facial expressions of the speaker automatically, e.g. smile when they smile, look sad when they look sad, etc. Did they notice this happening?

Watchpoints 1 Strict timing is important.

2 It is sometimes difficult for group members to think of anything to talk about, so suggestions like 'the best/worst thing' are helpful. Nothing too threatening should be introduced.

3 All feelings, however inappropriate they may seem to the listener, should be accepted. It is not helpful to say things like 'You mustn't feel guilty' or 'How can you let someone like that upset you?'

Variation Instead of pairs, triads can be formed. A triad consists of a couple sitting opposite each other while a third person sits at right angles and acts as an observer. The exercise proceeds in the same way but it is the task of the observer to report back to the listener the quality of their listening by giving specific feedback, e.g. 'Your eye contact was good. I think you encouraged her to say more by the way you nodded your head in agreement.'

Exercise 24   WHAT SORT OF LISTENER AM I?

Method   *Individually* members of the group should complete the following sentence as many times as they like.

I find it difficult to talk to ＿＿ about ＿＿.

General discussion   Compare lists of people you find it difficult to talk to and the areas of particular difficulty.

Give out the handout *Barriers to Good Listening* on p. 60 and allow time for it to be read.

Do members of the group recognize (a) themselves, (b) anyone on their list, when reading the description of the communication blocks?

If listening blocks inhibit effective communication, what helps it? Make a list and display it on a wall.

Exercise No. 25   LISTENING QUIZ

See p. 61.

Exercise 26   SELF-APPRAISAL

See p. 62.

Exercise 27   CASE STUDY: GARY

See p. 63.

Recommended resources   John Powell sj and Loretta Brady msw, **Why Am I Afraid to Tell You Who I Am?** (Fontana).

Gerard Egan, **You and Me** (Brooks/Cole).

Parents and Teenagers (Open University).

How well do I cope with conflict?

AIMS The group will:

1 **Recognize the difference between aggressive, compliant and assertive behaviour.**

2 **Be encouraged to think in terms of problem-solving as an effective method of dealing with conflict.**

3 **Practise the skills involved in assertive behaviour and constructive negotiation.**

How well do I cope with conflict?

INPUT Successful relationships are those that handle conflict well. Conflict is a normal part of learning to live with other people and, handled constructively, leads to better understanding, personal growth and intimacy. Yet most of us hate the idea of any kind of disagreement.

Instinctively, we react to conflict in three ways:

1 Flight 2 Freeze 3 Fight

We adopt characteristic positions:

The Ostrich Position: Ignore it. 'I don't want to know.'

The Push-over Position: Anything for a quiet life. 'Do what you like.'

The Punch-up Position: My way, whatever the cost. 'I don't give a damn what you think.'

Perhaps you see yourself acting fairly predictably in one of these ways, or maybe your reaction will depend on the circumstances or the people involved. But none of these methods — burying head in the sand, compliance, or aggression — can ever provide more than a short-term solution to disagreement, and all three will eventually prove ineffective. (See final unit.)

In this unit we are exploring another way of resolving conflict — through negotiating skills and the use of appropriate assertive behaviour. This involves looking for a solution that is agreeable and fair to both parties, one that meets their legitimate interests so that they both gain from the outcome rather than one winning and one losing. This is known as a *win/win situation*.

Looking for a solution requires hard work and involves concessions. It requires concentration, clear communication, accurate understanding and a deal of guts.

Exercise 28   CONFLICT

Brainstorm   Sample brainstorm

Anger	Labels	Need to win
Fight	Standing up for	Losing
Unpleasantness	yourself	Clearing the air
Opposition	Fear	Failure
Sarcasm	Resentment	
Abuse	'A high' excitement	

Input   Conflict can be constructive and positive and if handled intelligently cements friendships rather than destroying them. Let's look at three different ways of handling conflict:

1 Aggression   Aggressive behaviour is trying to get what you want regardless of others. Sarcasm, manipulation, bullying, threats and belittling other people are seen as legitimate means to an end: winning at any cost.

2 Compliance   Compliant behaviour is giving in to other people. It is not asking for what you want or expressing what you feel. Afraid of upsetting anyone, you expect others to mind-read what you want and are resentful when they do not.

3 Assertion   Assertive behaviour is saying openly and honestly what you think and feel about a situation. It is standing up for yourself but does not ignore the rights of others. It is being able to express feelings, both positive and negative, while acknowledging that others may feel differently about the same issue. It helps to achieve a solution where both parties gain something, i.e. a win/win situation rather than a win/lose one.

(Based on Hopson and Scally, *Life Skills*, no. 1.)

Exercise 29   WHAT'S MY STYLE?

Method   The group leader will need the resource sheet on p. 64 for this exercise. It gives the outline of three situations A, B and C, also the role-playing instructions for nine people.

Divide into groups of three, i.e. a triad, and label each triad A, B, or C. Each triad consists of two people with speaking parts who will ad lib their dialogue, and one observer whose task it is to monitor the interaction. Number each member of the triad 1, 2, or 3, in order to allot roles. No. 1 plays the female, no. 2 plays the male and no. 3 is the observer.

First the group leader reads out the situation and then hands out the various roles according to the allotted numbers. Following the triad pattern, the two role players sit facing each other with the observer sitting at right angles to obtain the best view for observing.

Allow five minutes for the first role-play, then rotate chairs and roles so that the observer and characters are different. Repeat this format until each member of the triad has had the opportunity to act as observer.

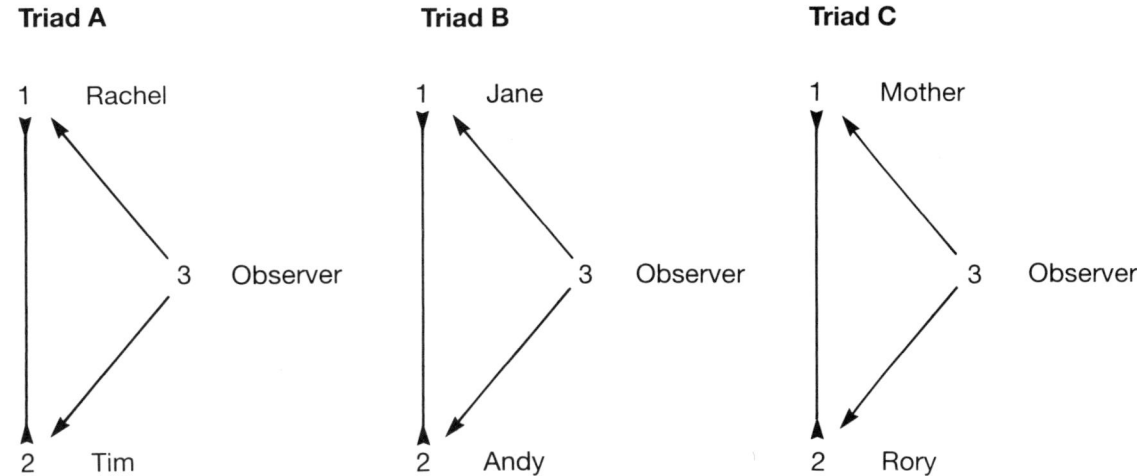

Triad A

1   Rachel

3   Observer

2   Tim

Triad B

1   Jane

3   Observer

2   Andy

Triad C

1   Mother

3   Observer

2   Rory

Main group Group leader has three large sheets of paper headed *Aggressive behaviour*, *Compliant behaviour* and *Assertive behaviour*. The observers can then feed back their findings. What kind of behaviour did they observe? Which headings do they think it should be written under? Does the rest of the group agree? Write it under the appropriate heading, e.g.

Aggression	*Compliance*	*Assertion*
Shouts	Placates	States own case
Wags finger	Whines	Listens
Threatens	Agrees	Suggests options
Bullies	Bows head	Relaxed posture

Make sure everyone has a chance to contribute before widening the discussion to explore the following questions:

Looking at the list, does it help us to understand the difference between aggression and assertion?

What is the difference? Can the group define (1) aggression, (2) assertion?

Is compliant behaviour effective? Why or why not?

Is assertive behaviour always appropriate?

If assertive behaviour is not always appropriate can you give specific examples of inappropriate assertiveness?

Is it harder to be assertive with some people rather than others?

With whom do you find it particularly difficult to be assertive? Make a list of difficult people from the group's individual contributions.

Exercise 30   LET'S MAKE THE MESSAGES ACCEPTABLE

Input

The group leader explains that some statements always provoke a defensive reaction. 'You' messages, for example, make a statement about the person to whom they are addressed. They are usually sweeping statements and contain words like 'always', 'never'. When they are critical they are experienced by the receiver as a personal attack and the instinctive response is to deny, defend or counter-attack.

It is helpful if, at this point, the group leader and a partner demonstrate a 'you' message and a typical reply, e.g.:

Statement: 'You are always so illogical.'
Reply: 'Well! You are a fine one to talk.'

An 'I' message, on the other hand, makes a statement about the sender. They offer information about me not you and describe what I feel, think, need or want. They are not accusatory and can be more easily accepted by the receiver than 'you' messages.

Group leader now demonstrates with the same partner an 'I' message and a typical reply, e.g.:

Statement: 'I feel really worried when I don't know you are going to be late.'
Reply: 'Sorry darling! I meant to phone but I was so busy I forgot all about it.'

Method

Split into pairs. The group leader gives out the resource sheet on p. 65 for the pairs to try out for themselves, to see how it feels to be on the end of a 'you' message. Allow two minutes. Check out with each couple how it felt.

    Now explain that the task of the pairs is to take it in turns to change the 'you' messages into 'I' messages. This involves putting themselves in the speaker's shoes and imagining how they feel, e.g. instead of 'You never treat me as an adult' a more assertive thing to say is 'I feel really frustrated when you treat me like a child'. Allow ten minutes.

Main group

How difficult was it to change 'You' messages into 'I' messages?

How did it feel to receive an 'I' message?

Do 'I' messages make it easier to communicate effectively in conflict situations?

Do they help to defuse the situation?

Would anyone in the group like to describe to the group any argument they have had recently. How did it develop? How could it have been handled more assertively?

Exercise 31 ROLE-PLAY SITUATIONS: TRYING IT OUT

Method

Divide into small groups (no more than six people). Group leader hands out the following list of people:

> Parents
> Friend
> Boy/girl-friend
> Person in authority, i.e. boss, teacher, etc.
> Official personnel, i.e. civil servants, etc.
> Someone you dislike.

She/he then asks each group to choose one of the list and devise a role-play involving a potential conflict situation e.g.
Parents.
Dolores wants to go with her friends to Italy for a fortnight's holiday. She is 17 and although her parents do not object to her having a holiday independent of the family, they are very worried about it being a mixed party. They don't know if they can trust them to behave responsibly. One of the boys has already had one run-in with the police. They are inclined to say no.

Allow 20 minutes to devise and allot role-play parts.

Each group then takes it in turn to present their role-play to the others. After each role-play the group should consider the following points:

How did each person feel in their role?
How difficult was it to be assertive?

Is it, in practice, more difficult to be assertive with some people rather than others?

How well was the potential conflict handled?

How was it handled well? Give specific examples.

How could it have been handled better? Give specific examples.

(NB: Do not forget to de-role after each role-play.)

Hand out 'How to improve your assertiveness skills' sheet on p. 66.

Exercise 32 HOW ASSERTIVE ARE YOU?

See p. 67.

Recommended resources

Barrie Hopson and Mike Scally, **Life Skills Programme No. 3** (Lifeskills Associates).

Tony Gough, **Couples Arguing** (Darton, Longman and Todd, 1987).

How at ease am I with my sexuality?

AIMS The group will:

1 Examine critically male and female stereotypes and look at some of their own assumptions, expectations and feelings towards the opposite sex.

2 Explore society's diverse and often confusing attitudes towards sexuality.

3 Clarify their own sexual values.

How at ease am I with my sexuality?

INPUT Outside influences — our parents, our friends, the culture we live in, our religion — affect the way we see the world. We are constantly exposed to a vast array of differing attitudes and opinions which reflect the pluralist society within which we live. Indoctrination, thankfully, is not only outmoded but ineffective. We are a questioning generation, suspicious of dogma and authority. Nevertheless, an essential part of growing up, one of the developmental tasks of adolescence (see Havighurst on p. 7), is the acquisition of a personal set of values: an ethical system as a guide to behaviour. This is difficult when there is no longer one accepted way of living and assorted values systems jostle to be heard. Nowhere is it more difficult than in the area of sexuality, as young people struggle to come to terms with their changing bodies, minds and emotions.

Sexuality has been defined as:

> *Our self-understanding and way of being in the world as male and female. It includes our appropriation of attitudes and characteristics which have been culturally defined as male and female. It involves our affectional orientation towards those of the same or opposite sex. It includes our attitudes about our own bodies and those of others.*
>
> (James B. Nelson, *Embodiment: An Approach to Sexuality and Christian Theology* (Augsburg Publishing, 1978))

Young people need to understand that their sexuality is central to their total identity. 'Who am I?' involves the totality of the person: physical, emotional, psychological and spiritual. Having sex with bodies without involving heads and hearts is not 'making love' but 'having sex'. The person is of no importance, and so becomes disposable like an object of little worth. Sexual morality ultimately rests on the way we respect and value other people — and that is intrinsically dependent on the way we respect and value ourselves.

Exercise 33 WHAT'S PROPER?

See p. 68.

Exercise 34 PINK FOR A GIRL, BLUE FOR A BOY

Two groups of equal size

Each group needs a large sheet of paper and a marker pen. Group A brainstorms the word *man* and group B brainstorms the word *woman*.

Sample brainstorms

Man		*Woman*	
Strong	Muscular	Cook	Parties
Good-looking	Hard	Weak	Marvellous
MCP	Hairy	Powerful	Demanding
Macho	Opportunities	Put-down	Periods
Tanned	Married	Frigid	Gossip
Violence	Women	Housewife	Sex object
Sex	Easy life	Seduction	Equal
Puny	Egotistical	Flirt	Sensitive
Pressure	Logical	Pregnancy	Love
Stubborn	Primitive	Emotional	Manipulative
Emotionally	Hard done-by	Caring	Bitchy
inept	Worker	Marriage	Children

Main group

Discussion:

What, if anything, do the two lists have in common?

What, if any, are the differences?

What attitudes are reflected in the lists towards (1) women? (2) men?

Do you think the attitudes reflected by this group are typical of society in general or not? If they are not typical, in what ways are they different?

How do you feel about (1) this group's attitudes towards women? (2) this group's attitudes towards men?

How do you feel about society's attitudes towards men and women?

Exercise 35

Single-sex groups

EXPECTATIONS

The male group brainstorms:
    As a man I am expected to be _____
    As a man I expect women to be _____

The female group brainstorms:
    As a woman I am expected to be _____
    As a woman I expect men to be _____

Responses are written on a large sheet of paper to be displayed on the wall at the end of the session.

Sample brainstorms

As a man I am expected to be:

Arrogant	Level-headed
Virile	Caring
A leader	Unemotional
Tough	Butch
Strong	Decisive
Protective	Firm
Initiator	Dominant
Practical	Supportive
Controlled	Drinker

As a man I expect women to be:

Attractive	Understanding
Sexy	Gentle
Good friend	Supportive
Homely	Wild
Fun	Interested in me
Faithful	Kind

As a woman I am expected to be:

Understanding	Passive
Domesticated	Unambitious
Feminine	A mother — and lump it
Sexually attractive	Subordinate
Emotional	Compassionate
Lady-like	Sympathetic
Aware	Gentle
Creative	Good hostess
Capable	Heart of the family

As a woman I expect men to be:

Good looking	Reliable
Intelligent	Kind
Strong	Amusing
Interesting	Rich
Sporty	Ambitious
Family-minded	Tender

Main group   Discuss:

Are men and women born equal but different, or are the differences merely a matter of upbringing? How equal is our society's treatment of men and women?

How do your own expectations affect the opposite sex? If you have a girl/boy-friend, have you ever discussed the expectations you have of each other?

To read out at end of session

'For every woman'

For every woman who is tired of acting weak when she knows she is strong, there is a man who is tired of appearing strong when he feels vulnerable.

For every woman who is tired of acting dumb, there is a man who is burdened with the expectation of 'knowing everything'.

For every woman who is tired of being called 'an emotional female', there is a man who is denied the right to weep and to be gentle.

For every woman who is called unfeminine when she competes, there is a man for whom competition is the only way to prove his masculinity.

For every woman who is tired of being a sex object, there is a man who must worry about his potency.

(Nancy R. Smith)

Exercise 36

Individual exercise

WHAT DO I THINK?

See sheet on p. 69.

Mixed pairs

To share their individual likes and dislikes. After enough time the couple can extend the discussion by joining with another pair.

Main group

Were you surprised by your partner's answers?

If so, why?

If not, why not?

What do you think are (1) the advantages of being a man? (2) the advantages of being a woman? (3) the disadvantages of being a man? (4) the disadvantages of being a woman?

Write the responses on to four large sheets of paper labelled 'Good news for men', 'Good news for women', 'Bad news for men', 'Bad news for women'.

Do sex roles affect relationships? Is there anything you would like to change in society's attitudes towards your own sex?

(NB: For a single-sex group these exercises would clearly need to be modified.)

Exercise 37

Single-sex groups

HOW DO I FEEL?

The female group brainstorms:
'As a woman I feel _____ '

The male group brainstorms:
'As a man I feel _____ '

The feeling words are then written on a large sheet of paper for the rest of the group to see.

Sample brainstorms

As a woman I feel:

Unsafe	Need to be needed
In control	Vulnerable
Frightened	Cheated — double standards
Longing to be loved	Dominant
Burdened	Ambitious
Annoyed	Confused
Inferior to men but confident	Taken for a ride
with women	Trapped
OK	Strong

As a man I feel:

Weak	Comfortable
Inadequate	Angry
Unsure	Powerful
Lonely	Great
Pressurized	Misunderstood
Jealous of women	Confused
OK	

Mixed pairs (if possible)

How easy/difficult did you find it to say how you felt about being male/female? Why do you think you found it easy/difficult?

Main group

Discuss:

1   Was it easier, in general, for the women or the men to say how they felt about their sexuality?

2   Do you think the role of women/men has changed for the better or the worse in the last 20 years?

3   If it were possible to change *one* thing only in society's attitude towards your own gender, what would it be?
List them.

4   Is there anything you can do to bring about these changes?

Exercise 38 SEXUAL MESSAGES

Four groups

As we grow up we are influenced by the spoken and unspoken messages about different aspects of our sexuality.

Group A will look at parental messages
Group B will look at peer group messages   about *sex*.
Group C will look at media messages
Group D will look at religious messages

A scribe can be appointed to write down the group's findings and report back to the main group.

Main group

Are any of the messages the same?

Are any of the messages different?
Have any of you changed any of your attitudes towards sex in the last five years?
What, if you have, persuaded you to do so?

This method can be used to explore a whole range of different issues, e.g. homosexuality, pornography, birth control, chastity, AIDS, pre-marital sex, child abuse, drugs etc. It also provides the opportunity to introduce correct information from such sources as the Health Education Council. In order to prevent boredom, rotate the groups so that they each have the opportunity to explore the issue from a different perspective.

Exercise 39   WHAT'S THE ATTRACTION?

Individual exercise

Everyone in the group chooses *one* only of the following sentences to complete:

I like having a girl/boy-friend because _____
I would like to have a girl/boy-friend because _____
I don't want a girl/boy-friend at the moment because _____

When you have chosen which sentence you wish to complete you should list ten reasons why:

You like having a girl/boy-friend.
You would like to have a girl/boy-friend.
You don't want a girl/boy-friend at the moment.

Main group

Discuss what, from your sentences, members of the group are looking for and what they fear from a relationship with a member of the opposite sex. List the *Hopes* and *Fears* on a board or flipchart.

Are any of your fears based on personal experiences?

Are any of your fears due to lack of confidence?

Are any of your fears founded on, real or supposed, lack of knowledge?

Having identified your fears can you think of ways to overcome them? *List them.*

Were you surprised by how alike/different your hopes were from other people's?

Would you say people generally wanted the same or different things from a relationship?

Was there a difference between what the men hoped for and what the women hoped for in a relationship?

As a group could you list what you think are the *three* most important things people are looking for in a relationship with the opposite sex?

What do you think helps to achieve a good relationship with the opposite sex?

Is it in any way different from what makes any good relationship?

Exercise 40   SEXUAL VALUES

Method   The group leader writes each of the following statements about sexual values on a separate piece of paper and pins them on to the wall. Group members are given time to walk around and look at each one. They may need a piece of paper and pen to put down their reactions. The group leader then invites them to do the individual task below.

'Sex is too special to squander.'

'The only sexual morality is to avoid having an unwanted baby.'

'Casual sex is OK as long as it is safe sex.'

'What does it matter as long as it is fun?'

'In sex you have the responsibility for another human being. That is some responsibility.'

'Do what you want to do.'

'The best sex is learnt within the security of marriage.'

'When two people are in love, what they do together is nobody's else's business.'

'Sex is a gift, with the potential for new life. How can it be treated lightly?'

'Sex is the most intimate human communication, an expression of love and a complete giving of self to another.'

'Celibacy before and fidelity after marriage is the only guarantee of safe sex.'

Individually   Choose the statement with which (1) you most agree, (2) you most disagree, (3) that makes you feel angry. Then find a partner and share the choices you have made and the reasons why you made them. If there is time, join another couple and share in a foursome.

Main group   Discuss the following:

How did you feel about making your choices? Why do you think you felt this way?

How did you learn about sex? Was it helpful or unhelpful? *List the things that were helpful/unhelpful.*

Did the way you learnt about sex affect your attitudes towards it?

Do any of you feel there are gaps in your sexual knowledge? Do you know where or to whom to go to get the necessary information?

What do you want your children to learn about sex?

How do you want your children to learn about sex?

Is there such a thing as 'safe sex'?

Exercise 41   WHY? WHY NOT?

Buzz groups   Each buzz group's task is to list (1) five reasons why you think people have pre-marital sex, (2) five reasons why you think people wait until they marry before they have sex.

All the reasons for or against should be collated from the groups and displayed for everybody to see.

Sample lists

For	*Against*
Makes you feel good +	Not ready +
It's fun +	Too special +
Curiosity –	Afraid –
Makes you feel adult –	Unwanted pregnancy –
To have a baby +	VD and AIDS –
Peer pressure –	Want marriage +
In love +	In love +
It's natural +	Hurt others +
Loss of partner –	Reputation –
Be left on shelf –	Against religion –
Everyone does it –	Feel guilty –
Effective contraception +	Feel cheap –
Prove you're not	More friends +
homosexual –	More fun +
Old-fashioned not to –	More wisdom +
To spite parents –	

Main group The group now decides from the displayed list which reasons they think should be rated as *positive* and which as *negative*. The positive reasons should be marked with a + sign and the negative reasons with a — sign (use different coloured markers).

Discuss How difficult it was to decide whether a reason was + or – ?

Does anyone want to change or challenge any of the +s or –s?

If instead of rating the reasons as positive or negative, the group rated the reasons as *mature* or *immature*, how would the ratings change?

Exercise 42 ## CASE STUDY: GERRY AND KATE

See p. 70.

Exercise 43 ## PROBLEM PAGE

Method The group should be encouraged to generate their own Problem Page and act as their own Agony Aunt. The samples on pp. 71–2 are intended to start them off, or to allow the group leader to introduce a particular topic if they wish it to be discussed.

Exercise 44 **CASE STUDY: RICHARD**

See p. 73.

Exercise 45 **CASE STUDY: TRACY**

See p. 74.

Exercise 46 **REFLECTIVE EXERCISE**

See p. 75.

Recommended resources

Religion, Ethnicity and Sex Education Pack (National Children's Bureau for The Sex Education Forum, November 1993).

Mary Porter and Gill Lenderyou, **Sex Education: Faith and Values** (Health Education Authority, 1993).

Robin Smith, **Living in Covenant with God and One Another** (World Council of Churches, 1992).

The Health of The Nation: HIV/Aids and Sexual Health (Department of Health, 1992).

Tom Williams and Rhona Hutchinson, **HIV Prevention: A Christian Response** (Archdiocese of St Andrews and Edinburgh).
Obtainable from: Community Education Officer, Gillis Centre, 113 Whithouse Loan, Edinburgh EH9 1BB.

AIDS: Working with Young People (AVERT, 1990).

Jo Frankham, **Not Under My Roof** (AVERT, 1992).

Both available from: AVERT (AIDS Education and Research Trust), 11 Denne Parade, Horsham, West Sussex RH12 1JD.

What does loving mean?

AIMS The group will:

1 Consider what society means by the word 'love'.

2 Discuss the differences and links between infatuation, romance and love.

3 Think about the qualities they are looking for in a sexual partner.

4 Clarify their own attitudes towards marriage.

5 Reflect upon what loving means to them in the light of their own needs and experience.

What does loving mean?

INPUT One of the most important questions, and one of the most confusing, is: what is love? 'How do I know if I am in love?' is the burning issue for most young people who have often experienced passionate feelings towards a member of the opposite sex, only to be appalled at their fleeting nature. The media bombard us with romantic images of instant love and easy loving; religion presents us with the ideal of fidelity, permanence and happy families; while our own experiences of the people around us present us with the hard reality of life. Is it any wonder that we are confused? Love is essential to the human condition, but is infinitely complex. It is a creative force, which, if misunderstood, neglected or abused, becomes wantonly destructive. Love is a paradox and we need to understand its enormous potential for human fulfilment or human misery.

Parents are responsible for our first lessons in love. It is the quality of parenting, the way we are held and cared for, that conveys that we are loved, are lovable, and that life itself is trustworthy. Children who receive this unconditional love usually grow up valuing themselves and other people and are able to give and receive love. They have a head-start in the development of a positive self-concept. But not everyone is so lucky. There are many parents who have themselves been deprived of love and so are unable to provide the necessary loving environment for their children. Love, like deprivation, works in cycles.

Much will also depend, as we grow up, on our experiences with other people, as they provide us with new models and new assessments of our self-image. Marriage, or a committed relationship, with its promise of permanence and fidelity, often provides a second chance and can have healing properties for those hurt by earlier relationships. We all need to love and be loved, at some time in our lives, otherwise we have difficulty in functioning as human beings.

Yet half the time we don't know what we are looking for and fail to recognize the real from the counterfeit. It is hardly surprising! The word 'love' is used in our language to describe the most trivial of emotions to the most intense.

Often we mistake infatuation for love, or romantic fantasies of Prince Charming or Ms Wonderful with real people. We dream of 'happy-ever-after' endings without appreciating the unrewarding chores of caring and loving. Sex can be, and often is, substituted for love and produces a misunderstanding and a diminishing of the true, creative, meaning of what it is to be loved and to love. Of course, love is a feeling. But it has to be much more than an emotional knee-jerk if it is to last.

Love is a choice; I choose you. Love is a decision; I will love you. Love is a commitment; I will love you for ever.

Exercise 47
Main group

WHAT DO WE MEAN BY LOVE?

A brainstorm on 'Love'.

Sample brainstorm

Caring	Pain/rejection	Unconditional
Loyalty	Possessiveness	Loneliness
Feeling secure/safe	Sacrifice	Acceptance
Generous	Home	Infidelity
Excitement	Parents	Children
Joy	Friends	Permanence
	Forgiving	

The group leader should check with the group that they agree that all the words listed in the brainstorm are loving.

Underline any that cause disagreement, e.g. infidelity, possessiveness.

Buzz groups

Each group will discuss and decide which five words on the brainstorm list they consider the most important aspects of loving. When they have reached agreement they may like to write their choices down to bring back with them into the main group.

Main group

Each buzz group reports back with its five words and a new list is collated on the flipchart.

Exercise 48 — WHAT ARE YOU LOOKING FOR?

Main group Think of all your relationships — parents, friends, opposite sex, future partner — and brainstorm what is it you are looking for, what is it you need from your relationships?

Sample brainstorm

Trust	Care	Recognition
Security	Acceptance	Children
Loyalty	Growth	Love
Friendship	Praise	To be special
Fun	Understanding	Space
Stimulation	Intimacy	Encouragement
Challenge	Sex	

Input The things we look for from other people are needs, not wants. We all need to be loved, and all the things we have listed here are what loving is about. Often, however, this goes unrecognized and unappreciated and we think about love in terms of romance and happy-ever-after endings. We are going to look at the source of some of our confusion.

Exercise 49 — LOVE MESSAGES

Divide into three groups *Group 1* will look at the messages they have received about love from their parents.

Group 2 will look at messages about love conveyed by TV, magazines, novels, etc.

Group 3 will look at what their religion says about love.

Each group will need a large sheet of paper on which to write their messages.

Main group Display the three sets of messages on a wall where everyone can see them. Invite each group to explain the messages they have written down to the rest of the group.

General discussion How easy/difficult was it to do this exercise?

How different were the messages about love?

How similar were the messages about love?

How many of the messages about love would you describe as romantic?

How many of the messages about love would you describe as idealistic?

How many of the messages about love would you describe as realistic?

How many of the messages have nothing to do with real love and are untrue?

Individual quiz

What's it all about?

Hand out the individual quiz on p. 76 for completion.

Divide into pairs to share and compare answers. If time allows, join up with another couple and continue the sharing as a foursome.

Group discussion

What is infatuation? Are there any warning signs to alert you to the fact that this is just a passing phase not the real thing?

What part does romance play in love?

Is love a feeling or a decision?

Are there any responsibilities involved in loving another person? If so, what are they?

The Greeks used to believe real love required three equally important elements: sexual attraction (*erōs*), friendship (*philia*), and caring (*agapē*). What do you think?

Exercise 50

WHAT IS IT YOU DON'T WANT?

Brainstorm

What characteristics would they *not* like their ideal girl/boy-friend to have?

Sample brainstorm

Meanness	Unforgiving	Nasty
Bad temper	Moody	Unfeeling
Laziness	Cruel	Selfish
Macho	Boring	Unsociable
Vocal feminist	Unloving	Snob
Sarcastic	Cold	Disgusting habits

Input

It is sometimes easier to know what you don't want rather than what you do want — particularly when it comes to the opposite sex. The next exercise is designed to start you thinking about what short of a partner you need to fit in with what you want out of life.

Exercise 51

WHAT IS IDEAL?

Method

Use the handout on p. 77 as a guide. Each individual is asked to choose the eight qualities they would most appreciate in an ideal boy/girl-friend. They should then rate them from 1 to 8 in descending order of priority.

In pairs

Share and compare choices together. If time allows join another couple to continue discussing the differences in your choices.

Group discussion	How difficult was it to choose and rate eight qualities? If you had been choosing a marriage partner would your choices have been the same?
Method	Repeat the Supermatch exercise, but this time choose the eight qualities they think they have and would bring into a relationship with the opposite sex.
Group discussion	What do you think would be the advantages of a partner who is temperamentally similar to yourself? Temperamentally different?
	What do you think would be the disadvantages of a partner who is temperamentally similar to yourself? Temperamentally different?
	Does your supermatch represent the attractions of likes or opposites? How do you feel about this?

Exercise 52   A BLESSING OR A CURSE?

Method	Give out the handout on p. 78.
General discussion	Which sentence did people choose as summing up what marriage is about for them? Write them on the flip-chart. Mark them with a + or a –, according to whether they are positive or negative.
	Were your attitudes towards marriage mainly positive or negative?
	What do you think colours an individual's view of marriage?
	Why do you think marriage is sometimes described as a second chance?

Exercise 53   CASE STUDY: JO

See p. 79.

Exercise 54   ROLE-PLAY: MARRIAGE MATTERS

See p. 80.

Exercise 55   WHY DO THEY DO IT?

Brainstorm   Any reasons you can think of why people get married.

Sample brainstorm

In love	Happiness
Care for each other	Share everything

Want to spend their lives together	Grow old together
Leave home	Can't imagine life without him/her
Have children	Trust her/him to love me always
Be a family	
Security	Pressure from family etc.

Buzz groups

Are there any reasons on the list that you consider wrong reasons for getting married? Can you think of any other reasons for getting married that would be unhelpful to the future marriage?

Sample 'wrong' reasons

Leave home	Pressure
To be recognized as an adult	Pity
On the rebound	Romance, e.g. 'She is perfect, the only woman in the world for me'
In order to change partner, e.g. 'He will be different once we are married'	
Pregnancy	Put the magic back into the relationship
Longing for a baby	Money
Fear of being left on the shelf	Unable to live alone
Desperation	

Main group

Compare lists and then collate into one list to be displayed on the wall so that everyone can see it.

General discussion

Every couple who marry think that their marriage will work. Apart from marriages that break down because people marry for the wrong reasons, what other external pressures (e.g. unemployment) can cause problems for a marriage?

What internal problems in the relationship (e.g. inability to express feelings etc.) will cause problems for a marriage?

The daily chores of caring for somebody else can be monotonous and unrewarding (e.g. looking after a baby, tending a sick wife). Would you agree that all loving involves a high degree of giving?

Exercise 56 CASE STUDY: SALLY AND ALAN

See sheet on p. 81.

An invitation to any of the helping agencies, e.g. Relate or CMAC, could be beneficial at this stage to talk about their work. It is important that the group become aware of the help available in relationship matters, and that they know where to go to obtain it.

Exercise no. 57 REFLECTION EXERCISE

See p. 82.

Exercise 58 WHAT IS MORALLY LOVING BEHAVIOUR?

Method   Give out or write up the sheet on p. 83.

Buzz groups   Each group takes one or two of the seven guidelines and decides what the word means, and its consequences in terms of practical behaviour. Make a list of self-liberating behaviour etc.

Main group   For general discussion:

Compare lists. How difficult did they find the task?

Do you agree that loving behaviour needs to be self-liberating, other-enriching etc.? If yes, why? If no, why not?

Do you want to add anything to the list or delete anything from the list? Give your reasons.

Individually or in small groups   See the second part of the sheet on p. 83.

Recommended resources   Daral Litvinoff, **The Relate Guide to Better Relationships** (Vermilion, 1991).

Jack Dominian, **The Capacity to Love** (Darton, Longman and Todd, reprinted 1986).

Michael Pennock, **Choosing: Cases in Moral Decision Making** (Ave Maria Press, 1991).

Jerome Trahey, **Building Self-Esteem: A Workbook for Teens** (Resource Publications Inc.).

Margaret Grimer, **Making Families Work** (Geoffrey Chapman, 1994).

Michele McCarthy, **Loving** (Wm. C. Brown).

Pinch/Crunch: making it work

AIMS   The group will:

1   Achieve a basic understanding of the model Pinch/Crunch.

2   Explore some of the hopes, fears and expectations experienced at the beginning of a new relationship.

3   Identify the people and situations they find the most difficult to cope with assertively, even if appropriate.

4   Practise further exercises in assertion and affirmation.

Pinch/Crunch: making it work

Input   The Pinch/Crunch model emphasizes the dynamic interaction within marriage or a long-term intimate relationship. When two people marry they bring into the relationship the whole of their past history, including the assumptions they make about life, the things they take for granted, their values and the behaviour they consider normal. Consciously and unconsciously they bring their needs and their fears, the acceptable and the unacceptable parts of themselves.

The 'honeymoon' period, however, never lasts. Assumptions and expectations will need to be modified. At no time is a relationship ever static; periods of stability are constantly challenged by internal and external changes to which the relationship must adapt in order to survive.

The purpose of this unit is to help group members to recognize danger points in a relationship and the need to solve problems before they become intractable.

Exercise 59

Main group

THE PINCH/CRUNCH MODEL

Hand out copies of the Pinch/Crunch model and explanation on pp. 84–6 (a large reproduction on the flipchart or OHP would be helpful). Talk the group through the various stages.

Divide into three groups

Group A will explore some of the *hopes* there are likely to be at the beginning of an intimate relationship.

Group B will explore some of the *fears* there are likely to be at the beginning of an intimate relationship.

Group C will explore some of the *expectations* there are likely to be at the beginning of an intimate relationship.

After 20 minutes the three groups should come together to share and discuss their findings.

Renegotiating expectations

Input Renegotiating expectations has four stages:

1 Recognize there is a pinch, own the feelings as belonging to you and decide to share them.

2 Disclose the feelings appropriately, i.e. choose the right words, the right time and place so that there is sufficient rapport between you to carry you through. There is a formula that goes '*When you — I feel — Because —*'.

3 Listen and respond to the feelings expressed. Offer your own feelings in return. Try to agree that there is a shared problem to be resolved.

4 Search together for a *win/win* solution. This indicates a shared commitment to maintaining the relationship.

Exercise 60 **THREE-PART MESSAGES**

One way of dealing with negative feelings in an assertive way is by using a three-part message. This is a better alternative to feeling angry and saying nothing, or giving vent to our feelings in an aggressive, uncontrolled manner.

It is a logical development of the 'I' messages used in an earlier unit.

Three-part messages are made up as follows:

Describe the behaviour
When you — (*followed by the pinch*)
Disclose the feeling
I feel — (*followed by negative feelings*)
Tangible effect
because — (*followed by the effect on you*).

Examples
When you borrow my shirts . . . I feel annoyed . . . because they have to be washed again.

When you arrive late . . . I feel upset . . . because I think you don't care.

When you repeated what I said ... I felt let down ... because I had told you in confidence.

Some rules

1 Avoid generalizing, sarcasm, exaggeration, put-downs or wind-ups, e.g. 'You are always late', 'You would, wouldn't you?', 'You make me sick'.

2 Don't send other people's three-part messages, only your own.

Into pairs

1 Take it in turns to think of a pinch you have experienced. Write out a three-part message and discuss it with your partner. Practise saying out loud the sentences you have scripted and ask your partner for their reaction. Continue practising the same sentence until you feel comfortable with it and your partner agrees it sounds OK.

2 Now you are going to practise how to cope with the negative feelings of other people when they are directed towards you. We usually meet aggressiveness with aggressiveness or with resentful defensiveness. This is a way of avoiding the defend/attack spiral without feeling you are running away. It is not a magic formula but it can work.

Hand out the drill on p. 87.

Exercise 61   HOW ASSERTIVE AM I?

Method

Hand out the Assertiveness Self-Assessment Questionnaire on p. 88.

Group members complete their own self-assessment table and then discuss in the group the following:

1 How easy/difficult was it to complete your self-assessment table?

2 Was there any particular group of people with whom the majority of you find it difficult to assert yourselves? If yes, why do you think this is?

3 Which was the most difficult: expressing positive feelings, standing up for yourself, or expressing negative feelings?

4 What makes it difficult to (a) express positive feelings, (b) stand up for yourself, (c) express negative feelings?

Into pairs

Take it in turns to choose one person from the assertiveness table and think of a fairly recent disagreement you have had with them. Share it with your partner, then discuss how you could have handled it better. (NB: Only share what is appropriate.)

Exercise 62   PRAISE

Into pairs

Help each other to remember an occasion when you failed to tell someone the good feelings you had as a result of something they had done or said, e.g. you failed to praise someone who deserved praise. What prevented you? Has the opportunity been lost or can you still tell them?

Now think of something you like about your partner and tell them what it is you like. Ask them how they feel about what you have said. Tell them how you feel about what they like about you.

Final exercise

Method The group leader hands out sheets of paper and safety pins and gets group members to pin a sheet on to somebody else's back (including group leader's). When everyone has a sheet of paper attached to their back the task is for everybody to mill around and write something they like about each person on their back. Whatever the number of the group should be the number of good comments on each back. The noise and bustle is part of the fun. At the end of the exercise everyone should be invited to take the sheets off their backs, to read them and take them home. It can be suggested that they hide them in a drawer and take them out if ever they need a boost to their self-esteem.

Pinch/Crunch was adapted from John J. Sherwood and John J. Scherer, *The Dating Mating Game: How to Play Without Losing* (Purdue University, 1974).

The Assertiveness Self-Assessment Questionnaire was adapted from Colleen Kelly, *Assertion Training: A Facilitator's Guide* (University Associates, 1979).

Three Part Messages was adapted from Robert Bolton, *People Skills* (Prentice-Hall, 1979).

Recommended resources Richard Nelson-Jones, **Human Relationship Skills**, 2nd edition (Cassell, 1990).

Margaret Grimer, **Making Marriage Work** (Geoffrey Chapman, 1987).

MIRROR IMAGE

Imagine a three-part mirror. The central panel reflects you as you see yourself now; the left-hand mirror reflects you as you were; and the right-hand one as you would like to be in ten years' time.

Me at 13 years	Me now	Me in ten years' time

Either in words or symbols describe yourself as you appear in each panel of the mirror.

How have you changed since you were 13?

What changes will you have to make to achieve this?

What have you lost? What have you gained?

What do you see as your biggest hurdles?

How do you see yourself in ten years' time?

Find a partner and describe your mirror to them. Listen while they tell you about themselves. If there is time, join up with another couple to make a foursome and continue talking about yourselves, learning more about the other three.

GETTING TO KNOW ME

I think what my friends most like about me is _____

I feel most confident when _____

I wish people would _____

I wonder _____

I worry about _____

I see myself as _____

I am best at _____

I am learning to _____

I enjoyed _____

My favourite star is _____

I want to be _____

I look forward to _____

I don't like _____

I'm not afraid to _____

My favourite TV programme is _____

I am happiest when _____

I am getting better at _____

I get hurt when _____

I am glad that _____

HOW DO I SEE MYSELF?

This is a personal exercise, not to be shared unless you wish to do so. You only have 15 minutes to complete the sentences; so don't agonize about it, just write down what immediately springs to mind.

I am _____

I am _____

I am _____

I am _____

I am _____

I am _____

I am _____

I am _____

I am _____

I am _____

Activity

1 Go through your list of sentences and mark each one with a + or – depending on whether you consider it a positive or negative statement. Add up your positives and negatives.

2 Examine your self-esteem by counting the number of positive statements you have made. What sort of shape is it in? Give yourself a rating by putting a mark at the most appropriate place on the following line.

Low   Average   High

3 Look back through your sentences and cross out those which, on reflection, you don't think are very important.

Then complete the following sentences:

I learnt that I _____

I realize that I _____

I was disappointed that I _____

I was pleased that I _____

4 What can you do to improve your own and other people's self-esteem?

REFLECTIVE EXERCISE

(Not for sharing)

I get angry with myself when _____

I like myself best when _____

I feel ashamed when _____

I feel on top of the world when I _____

I'm disappointed with myself when _____

When I fail, I feel _____

I feel down when _____

I feel confident when _____

When I do things I think are wrong, I _____

I'm most at peace with myself when _____

I get depressed when _____

When I think of the past I _____

When I look at the future I _____

I think I am OK when _____

I am not sure I am OK when _____

I think I need to _____

What does this exercise tell you about yourself?

WHAT'S IN A FACE?

Look at the photographs and then answer the following question:

Which of these people would you choose to be your uncle or aunt?

CASE STUDY: MARIKA

Marika met Joseph at a local disco. She had been feeling a bit spare when he came over to speak to her. She liked him immediately. He made her laugh and the evening was fun. They started to go out together and things were fine. One day Marika asked him to come round to her house to collect her before they went out. She really wanted her Mum to meet him. She had told her about him and now she wanted to show him off. Joseph arrived on time but he hardly said a word. He looked embarrassed and even a bit shifty. Marika couldn't wait to get him out of the house. She knew what her Mum was thinking even though she tried to be friendly. She wasn't prepared for the outburst, however, that took place on her return home. She hadn't had a very good night. Joseph had been moody, quite unlike his usual self. When she asked him why he hadn't been more friendly with her mother, he said 'What's the point? She didn't like me. I think she is a right snob.' Marika was angry. But she was even more upset when she got home and her mother launched into her. 'I can't think what you see in him. Those awful clothes! And his hair was disgusting. Why does he wear it so long? He looks a real layabout. I wouldn't be at all surprised if he wasn't on drugs.'

Marika's Mum tried to be friendly, so why did Joseph think she was a snob? How did Joseph feel?

Why did Marika's Mum react so badly to Joseph? How did she feel?

Is the way we dress a statement about who we are?

Is there anything Marika can do to change (a) Joseph's first impressions of her mother? (b) her mother's first impressions of Joseph?

How often do you change your first impressions of people? Can you remember specific examples?

Is it ever possible to know what people are really like? Which is the best guide: the way they dress, what they say, or the way they behave?

CASE STUDY: JENNY

Jenny is on a strict diet and is driving her family mad. Every mealtime is a nightmare. Her father loses his temper and Jenny always ends up in tears. 'It isn't as if you were fat', said her mother, 'I could understand it then, but you are nicely proportioned. I wish I had your figure.' 'Well, nobody else does', wailed Jenny. 'I need to lose at least two stone.' Jenny's mother was horrified. Jenny was tall and big-boned. If she lost two stone she would look anorexic. She was already looking pale and pinched and seemed to have no enthusiasm for anything. All she could think about was her weight. How could she be so stupid?

Is Jenny stupid? How is she feeling?

Why is her diet so important to her?

If you were Jenny's mother, would you be worried?

How could Jenny's parents help her to get a sense of proportion about her figure?

Is it more acceptable to be overweight if you are a man rather than a woman? Why/ why not?

Body image is linked to self-esteem, i.e. the way we value ourselves. Where do we get our stereotypes of male and female body images from? Why do we try to conform to them, often at the expense of our health?

What does it feel like when people make fun of your appearance?

What can you do to make the most of how you look and adopt a positive attitude to your own bodies?

REFLECTIVE EXERCISE

(Not to be shared)

The best thing about meeting new people is _____

The worst thing about meeting new people is _____

When I compare myself with other people I _____

Most people think I _____

People hurt me when _____

I think I hurt other people when I _____

I feel awkward and out of place when _____

My friends like me because _____

What I like best about myself is _____

When I meet new people I am usually _____

I feel at my best with people when _____

Looking at your answers: (a) How comfortable are you in new company? (b) How good are you at making other people feel comfortable in your company? (c) What do you need to do to become more open to other people?

BARRIERS TO GOOD LISTENING

Advice
Just do as I say. How you feel doesn't come into it.

Competition
Mental measuring: while you talk I am busy looking you up and down and comparing you unfavourably with me.

Distraction
Impatient or uncomfortable with listening. Distractions come easily to the rescue. 'Sorry, what were you saying?'

Switch off
It is easy to opt out of a conversation and effortlessly drift into your own thoughts, dreams or fantasies. Glassy eyes and a far-way expression are dead give-aways.

Red flag
An automatic response to trigger words in the conversation because of own strong feelings on the subject. Danger zones are religion, politics, education. Can you add to the list?

Poor me
Preoccupation with 'poor me' means listening is impossible because of obsession with self. Negative thoughts and collecting grievances are automatic. 'It's all right for you, what about me?'

Identification
'That reminds me of . . .' I can't wait for the opportunity to rush in with my own fascinating stories. 'Turn the spotlight back on me quick.'

Ignoring
Listens but fails to respond. Gives away no clue to inner reactions or feelings.

Labelling
Who I think you are stops me listening to you. Put people into categories and make instant judgements. Jewish? Black? English? old? etc., etc. Why listen to them?

Placating
Agreeing with everything is very pleasant even if it isn't honest or helpful.

Rehearsal
Thinking about my all-important reply takes my mind off listening to you.

Sarcasm
Guaranteed to stop any communication.

LISTENING QUIZ

How much do you know about the art of listening? Answer 'true' or 'false' to each of these statements:

1   Your thoughts can interfere with your listening.

2   You may resist listening to others who criticize, blame or get angry with you.

3   You are more likely to talk to those with whom you feel safe than with those with whom you do not.

4   If you have something you can't wait to say you are likely to be a good listener.

5   Some people use listening as an excuse for not revealing anything about themselves.

6   If you are feeling emotional about an issue you are likely to listen more attentively to other people.

7   Angry people are rarely good listeners.

8   Talking is more important than listening.

9   You are less likely to hear messages which agree with your view of yourself than messages that challenge that view.

10   Fatigue never affects the quality of your listening.

How to score

1 True; 2 True; 3 True; 4 False; 5 False; 6 False; 7 True; 8 False; 9 False; 10 False.

Give yourself two points for each correct answer. If you score 16 or more you have a good understanding of the art of listening. A score of ten or less would suggest you need to improve your listening skills. The chances are you are missing a lot of clues and useful information.

SELF-APPRAISAL

Think of one person on your list of those whom you are finding it difficult to get on with at the moment. Ask yourself the following questions:

1   Do I really want to improve this relationship?

2   Do I try to listen?

3   Do I try to understand how they feel?

4   Have I ever tried to put myself into their shoes and see their point of view?

5   Do I ever tell them how I feel?

6   Do I show that I respect them and value what they say?

7   Do I ever admit that I may be at fault or in the wrong?

8   Do I ever thank, compliment or praise them?

9   How much effort have I made to improve this relationship?

10   How much more effort do I need to make to improve this relationship?

Looking at your answers, how do you think you can improve your communication with other people?

Active listening can be facilitated by remembering the following:

Six golden rules

1   SOLER rules OK!
2   Stop talking, including internal and mental chatter, and don't interrupt.
3   Relax. Tension and anxiety reduces the ear's ability to hear.
4   Listening is about understanding, not winning arguments.
5   Don't let personal prejudices affect your response to what you hear.
6   Listening is an activity. It requires time and concentration.

CASE STUDY: GARY

IF ONLY I COULD TALK TO SOMEONE

Gary is in his first term at university and finding it hard going. Everyone else in his tutor group seems fairly casual about work but he is worried about his ability to keep up. He was considered bright at school and took A levels in his stride. Now he is all at sea. He won't admit to feeling homesick but even coping with his own washing seems an insurmountable problem. But worst of all, he is worried sick about his parents. He had been glad to get away from all the bickering and tension. Last night on the telephone his mother had said she couldn't stand it any more. She had been crying and he had felt so helpless. He loved his father and hated having to take sides. He was sure that they would eventually divorce and, old as was, he couldn't bear it. Why were they both so selfish? Why didn't they ever think of him or his younger sister? Poor Gemma! It must be even worse for her.

He felt like chucking the whole thing in and getting a job as far away as possible from everybody and everything. If only there was somebody he could trust . . .

How is Gary feeling?

How would having somebody he could trust help Gary?

Would it help anyone if Gary threw up his university career?

What does Gary need to do?

If you were Gary's friend what could you do to help him?

Is Gary's reaction to his parents' relationship breakdown typical or not?

Who else needs help in this situation? To whom could they go to get help?

If you had a problem where would you go to get help? Take a few minutes to think about your own support system. If you have no close family or friends, where might you look for support?

WHAT'S MY STYLE?

Situation A

Rachel and Tim are trying to arrange a holiday together. They have a pile of brochures but they can't seem to agree on anything. Tim's idea of the perfect holiday is an isolated beach and plenty of sun. Rachel burns easily, hates the thought of a beach holiday and wants to go somewhere with a bit of culture and lots to do and see. Something or somebody has got to give. Will it be Rachel or Tim?

Situation B

Jane is fed up with her boy-friend Andy. Whenever they arrange to meet he is always late. She hates standing about in a public place with everybody looking at her. He says there is nothing he can do about it. He is a medical student working in the teaching hospital and can often be delayed through no fault of his own. Something or somebody has got to change. Will it be Jane or Andy?

Situation C

Rory is determined to go to the weekend music festival with his friends. His mother is equally determined to stop him. Something or somebody has to bend. Will it be Rory or his mother?

Triad A

No. 1 You are Rachel. You want an active and exciting holiday.
No. 2 You are Tim. You want a beach holiday.
No. 3 You are the observer. Your task is to observe how Rachel and Tim resolve their problem. Check (a) what they say, (b) their body language, (c) their general approach. Jot down on paper what strikes you the most.

Triad B

No. 1 You are Jane. You are fed up with Andy for his lack of punctuality.
No. 2 You are Andy. You can't understand why Jane doesn't understand the difficulty you have with your work.
No. 3 You are the observer. Your task is to observe how Jane and Andy resolve their problem. Check (a) what they say, (b) their body language, (c) their general approach. Jot down on a piece of paper what strikes you the most.

Triad C

No. 1 You are Rory's mother. You don't want Rory to go to the music festival in case he gets into trouble.
No. 2 You are Rory. You are determined to go to the music festival with your friends.
No. 3 You are the observer. Your task is to observe how Rory and his mother resolve their problem. Check (a) what they say, (b) their body language, (c) their general approach. Jot down on a piece of paper what strikes you the most.

'YOU' MESSAGES

'You make me sick.'

'You always take me for granted.'

'You never do anything to help in the house.'

'You promised not to tell anybody.'

'You never stop nagging.'

'You are such a bore!'

HOW TO IMPROVE YOUR ASSERTIVENESS SKILLS

1   Assertiveness is a valuable skill but must be used appropriately. Being constantly assertive is counter-productive and raises hackles. Decide on your priorities and how important an issue is to you before opting to make a stand on it.

2   Know what you want or do not want and state it clearly. If your body language does not match your verbal message, you will be sending conflicting signals, so stand up straight, use direct eye contact, avoid nervous gestures and stay calm!

3   Try to choose the right time to raise an issue.

4   Say what you like and value about the person or situation before saying what you don't like and want changed.

5   Be specific. Don't make vague statement, e.g. 'You expect too much of me', but explain the situation, e.g. 'I can't pass my exams and go out with you every night.'

6   Be prepared to acknowledge your thoughts and feelings. Make 'I' statements, not 'you' statements.

7   Listen and be receptive to the other person's point of view.

8   Don't expect to get it all your own way. Look for a solution acceptable to both parties.

9   Don't pretend to understand if you don't. Ask for clarification, e.g. 'Do you mean . . .', 'What was it I said that upset you?'

10 Don't be afraid of physical contact, if appropriate. Touching is an important means of communication and can reassure and comfort when words are inadequate.

HOW ASSERTIVE ARE YOU?

Think of disagreements you have had in the past and answer the following questions, as honestly as possible, by ticking either Yes or No.

Do you tend to say words like 'never', 'always', 'everybody' when you argue?

Yes/No

Do you think 'If he/she/they loved me, they would know how I feel?'

Yes/No

Do you often cover up your real feelings by saying 'It doesn't matter' when it does, or 'I'm fine' when you are not?

Yes/No

Do you sometimes make accusing statements like 'You started it' or 'It is all your fault'?

Yes/No

Do you make value statements like 'You can't do that'?

Yes/No

Do you deliberately hurt or belittle with comments like 'Trust you! You are hopeless!'

Yes/No

Do you state your opinions as if they are proven facts, e.g. 'Vegetarians are stupid'?

Yes/No

When you get upset, is it usually about 'the same old things'?

Yes/No

Do you react badly to criticism, even if it's justified? Do you find it difficult to apologize?

Yes/No

When you are upset about something, do you usually tell everyone else about it rather than the person concerned?

Yes/No

Count the number of *Yes* ticks, then ask yourself the 20-dollar question: are you good at resolving conflict or do you need to change your approach?

WHAT'S PROPER?

Are you comfortable, uncomfortable, or unsure about the following behaviour? Mark each sentence with either a C, a UC or an NS.

C = comfortable, UC = uncomfortable, and NS = not sure.

1　Women who ask men out.

2　Men who knit.

3　Women who play rugby or football.

4　Men who enter body-building contests.

5　Women who pose as Page 3 models.

6　Men who expect their girl-friends to share all the expenses when they go out together.

7　Women executives.

8　Men who wear make-up or have their hair permed.

9　Women who have strong views about life and love a good argument.

10　Men who act tough and like to win.

11　Women priests.

12　Men who join aerobics classes.

Buzz groups

Share your responses. Did any of your own or other people's answers surprise you? Did you feel strongly about any of your own or other people's responses?

Group discussion

Do you think expectations of behaviour (sex role stereotyping) limit: (1) women? (2) men? (3) both sexes?

If yes, why? If not, why not?

WHAT DO YOU THINK?

Complete the following sentences:

Women

I like a man who _____

I think men should _____

I would like a man who _____

I do not like men who _____

I think what a man most looks for in a woman is _____

I think it would be better if men _____

In my family the 'girls' _____

The thing I hate most about being a woman is _____

The thing I like most about being a woman is _____

I feel disappointed if men _____

I envy men when _____

I expect men to _____

Men

I like a woman who _____

I think women should _____

I would like a woman who _____

I do not like women who _____

I think what a woman most looks for in a man is _____

I think it would be better if women _____

In my family the 'boys' _____

The thing I hate most about being a man is _____

The thing I like most about being a man is _____

I feel disappointed if women _____

I envy women when _____

I expect women to _____

CASE STUDY: GERRY AND KATE

'IF YOU LOVE ME . . .'

Kate thinks: They should prove their love for each other by not having sex until they are married.

She says: If you loved me you wouldn't ask because I would feel: unsure, frightened, pressurized, worried, guilty. I think it is too important. Love is more than just sex. I want it to mean we belong to each other. I want other people to share in our happiness. I want to be open and honest, not hidden and furtive.

It would:
- Make me doubt your commitment to me and wonder if you really love me.
- Make me feel on trial.
- Start us off the wrong way.

Gerry thinks: They should prove their love for each other by having sex.

He says: If you loved me you would because I would feel: lovable, wanted, proud, right, physically good. I think if you loved me you would. If anything went wrong you know I would never let you down. If our relationship doesn't work out we will always be friends and know we really loved each other once.

It would:
- Show you are mine.
- Help me love you properly.
- Reassure me you are not frigid.
- Show I am a real man.
- Improve our relationship.
- Make me one of the boys.
- Prove my virility.

Main group discussion

What does Gerry need from a relationship with Kate?
What does Kate need from a relationship with Gerry?
What does Gerry fear from a relationship with Kate?
What does Kate fear from a relationship with Gerry?
If you were Kate's best friend what would you advise her to do?
If you were Gerry's best friend what would you advise him to do?
What effect do you think it will have on their future relationship if Kate agrees to pre-marital sex? If she doesn't?

Role-play

Role-play the same situation but reverse the roles so that Kate thinks they should have sex and Gerry thinks they should wait until they can marry. Would they use the same reasoning or would it be different?

PROBLEM PAGE

Samples

'I am short and fat and spotty. I hate the way I look, how could anyone ever fall in love with me? My friends think I don't care because I make jokes about it, but really I am very miserable.

'Sometimes I hate them, even though it is my own fault that they laugh at me. I have tried to diet but am too weak-willed. Sometimes I despair of ever leading a normal life. Please help me.'

'I feel abused and let down. My boy-friend and I have been going out together for three months and I honestly thought I loved him. Last night we were petting as usual when things got out of hand. I tried to stop him but he wouldn't and I wasn't strong enough to make him. Afterwards he said he was sorry but I'd only myself to blame for leading him on. I feel awful. I feel as if I have been raped and I never want to have anything to do with him again. I want to talk to someone, but I am afraid. They are bound to blame me and think I am a slag. What can I do?'

'My upbringing instilled in me the idea of a committed relationship. I am expected to meet a nice boy and settle down and raise a family. No problem, except I am not attracted to men. I am a lesbian and want to share my life with another woman. I have tried going out with men but it is no good. Frankly the thought sickens me. Yet I want exactly the same things as everybody else: love, fidelity and commitment. What chance do I have of personal happiness when I am afraid to express my true feelings?'

'Why is life so unfair? I was very upset when my boy-friend split up with me after more than a year. Since then I have been out with quite a few boys, even though I am not really interested in them.

'Jean, my best friend, says people are talking about me and calling me names. What can I do? It is horrible staying at home while everyone else is out enjoying themselves.'

'This is going to sound crazy but here goes! I am just an ordinary bloke. My friends say I am good-looking and girls do seem to fancy me. They even phone to ask me out — but you won't believe this — they terrify me. I don't know anything about women, being the only child of middle-aged parents. I would love to have a girl-friend but I don't know what is expected from me. What do women want from a man? Hearing males talk, you would think they were only after one thing.'

PROBLEM PAGE continued

'Please can you help me? Mac and I are in love and have made plans to get married next year. We have told each other everything about our past and I know Mac has had only one serious relationship before me. What worries me is that he said the relationship broke up because she became addicted to drugs and he couldn't cope. Now I am terrified about HIV and AIDS. Am I being silly? Could his ex-girl-friend have passed on the virus? Should I insist he gets tested for HIV? What do you think?'

'I feel so ashamed and I am worried I may be doing myself harm. My friends say it isn't a problem but I was taught it was sinful. Can you tell me the facts about masturbation? Do you think it is harmful? Do you think it is wrong?'

'How can I tell you how miserable I feel? I am pregnant by a boy I love very much. He loves me too, but we are too young to marry and have no money or anywhere to live. Abortion has always seemed wrong to me but what else can we do? Our parents would be horrified if they knew. I think mine would try to persuade me to keep the baby but my boy-friend would want an abortion anyway. There would be an awful row and I can't stand it. Feeling sick all the time doesn't help. Please tell me you understand and what I am doing is the best thing.'

CASE STUDY: RICHARD

Mark and Clare had looked forward to the weekend so much. Their son, Richard, was arriving back from America after three months away. He arrived looking fit and happy and asked if it was all right if his friend, Terry, joined them the next day to celebrate his return. 'I want you to get to know each other.' Lunch was a great success. Terry was amusing company and Richard was obviously delighted to be back home. It came as a terrible shock, therefore, when Richard announced that he and Terry were lovers and were going to live together. Until that moment they had no idea that their son was homosexual.

How do you think Richard's father reacted? How did he feel?

How do you think Richard's mother reacted? How did she feel?

Would your reaction have been different if Richard and Terry had been girls? If yes, why? If not, why not?

What would be their fears about Richard and Terry's relationship?

Do you think these fears are legitimate?

How important do you think his parents' reaction is to Richard?

How will he feel if his parents (a) refuse to have Terry in the house? (b) accept his decision while expressing their reservations? (c) welcome Terry as a new member of the family?

How would you feel if Richard was your brother? Why?

If you, or one of your friends, were worried about your sexual feelings, is there anyone or anywhere you could go to, for help and guidance?

Do you feel society's attitude towards homosexuality is justified or unjust? Give reasons. If opinions are divided a debate, with those who support and those who oppose society's attitudes, could be arranged with time given to prepare their arguments.

CASE STUDY:TRACY

Tracy is 14 years old and lives with her mother and her mother's boy-friend. She sees her own father only rarely, as he is usually at sea, and her only relations are living in Sheffield which is miles away. Her favourite teacher, Miss Lewis, has noticed that Tracy has become withdrawn and very quiet. She becomes increasingly worried about her. One day Tracy hangs back after the others have gone home. 'Do you want to see me, Tracy?', Miss Lewis asks. 'No Miss', says Tracy, then promptly bursts into tears. After much persuasion Tracy says she will tell her if she promises not to tell anyone else. Miss Lewis has no time to reply before Tracy bursts out, 'It's Bill, my Mum's boy-friend, he keeps trying to interfere with me. I've tried to tell Mum but she won't listen. I don't want to cause trouble but I don't know what to do. I thought you might be able to help me, but you did promise not to tell anyone else, didn't you?'

How is Tracy feeling?

How is Miss Lewis feeling?

Why do you think Tracy's mother doesn't want to know?

Is Miss Lewis bound to respect confidentiality or not?

What responsibility would Miss Lewis have if she said nothing and Bill went on abusing Tracy?

What can Miss Lewis do to help Tracy?

What do you think will happen as a consequence of Tracy telling Miss Lewis?

If you had been in Tracy's position, what would you have done?

REFLECTIVE EXERCISE

(Personal to the individual)

This is a private exercise to help you think through some of your own sexual feelings. It is not necessary to use a pen or paper. Just find a place to think through your answers on your own.

What makes me feel good about being a woman/man?

Are there gaps in my knowledge about sex? Do I know how to find out what I am unsure about?

Am I easily turned on by members of the opposite sex? Does this worry me?

Am I sometimes attracted to people of my own sex? Does this worry me?

Have I seen or heard anything about sex that has left a lasting impression? Is it a happy or unhappy one?

Is there any experience or unpleasant memory which still disturbs me and affects my attitude towards sex?

Is there anyone I trust enough to talk to about my sexual fears or anxieties?

WHAT'S IT ALL ABOUT?

Show which of the following statements you agree/disagree with by ticking the *Yes* or *No* column.

You can fall in love at first sight.	*Yes/No*
You can love someone but not like them.	*Yes/No*
There is only one person with whom I can fall in love.	*Yes/No*
If you love someone you can change them.	*Yes/No*
Love only involves the heart not the head.	*Yes/No*
Love is giving.	*Yes/No*
Love is a feeling and an instinct.	*Yes/No*
The more in love you are, the more you have to share with other people.	*Yes/No*
Jealousy is a sign of love.	*Yes/No*
You're in love if your tummy does somersaults every time you see her/him.	*Yes/No*
Love is a decision.	*Yes/No*
The best basis for love is friendship.	*Yes/No*
Physical attraction can be instant, love requires time.	*Yes/No*

SUPERMATCH

Ambitious (hard-working, aspiring)

Broadminded (open-minded)

Capable (competent, effective)

Cheerful (light-hearted)

Clean (neat, tidy)

Courageous (standing up for your beliefs)

Forgiving (willing to pardon others)

Helpful (working for the welfare of others)

Honest (sincere, truthful)

Imaginative (daring, creative)

Independent (self-reliant)

Intellectual (intelligent, reflective)

Logical (consistent, rational)

Loving (affectionate, tender)

Obedient (dutiful, respectful)

Polite (courteous, well-mannered)

Responsible (dependable, reliable)

Self-controlled (restrained, self-disciplined)

MARRIAGE QUOTES

Individually, read the different quotes about marriage. If you agree with them put a tick by their side. If you disagree put a cross, and if you are undecided put a question mark.

1   Marriage is old-fashioned: an out-of-date institution.

2   Marriage is a committed and healing relationship. It helps people to grow.

3   There is no difference between being married and living together.

4   Marriage, no matter how happy, is invariably a disappointment.

5   Marriage is the daily assurance that we are loved, even by someone who knows all our weaknesses.

6   Marriage provides the bedrock for family life.

7   Marriage is necessary for the stability and health of the nation.

8   Marriage? If you are a woman, forget it!

9   Marriage offers, for most people, the greatest potential for fulfilment and human happiness.

10   Marriage is well called a bond: it is slavery, the end of all personal freedom.

Choose the *one* sentence that best sums up for you what marriage is about.

CASE STUDY: JO

Jo had been living with Stephen for eight years. She thought they were happy and that he loved her. She could not believe it when he told her he was moving out of the flat which they rented together. Her best friend's reaction was immediate. She hugged her and said reassuringly 'Thank goodness you weren't married. At least you will save a fortune in legal fees.' Her mother said, also sympathetically, 'The next time you set up house with a man, you want to make quite sure you have a ring on your finger. I told you you were asking for trouble.'

How does Jo feel?

How helpful are the remarks of (a) her best friend, (b) her mother?

Is the break-up of couples who live together less painful than if they were married? If yes, why? If not, why not?

What is the difference, if any, between living together and marriage?

ROLE-PLAY: MARRIAGE MATTERS

Andrea and Ray are in love and plan to marry this year. They are the first of their crowd to 'take the plunge', although they are both in their mid-twenties. Everyone was delighted to hear the good news, except for John, Jenny, Denise and Phil who cannot understand why they don't live together first. What can Andrea and Ray say to convince them that they think their decision is the right one for them?

Method
Allot parts for role-play.

Andrea is in love with Ray and wants to spend the rest of her life with him 'for better for worse, for richer for poorer, in sickness and in health, till death do us part', because ——

Ray is in love with Andrea and wants to share his life with her always because ——

John doesn't believe in marriage. He thinks it is a waste of time and a waste of money. If you love each other you don't need a public ceremony to prove it.

Jenny is afraid marriage is too risky. Her parents were divorced and she thinks that if you live together and then split up it would be less painful emotionally and financially. If you are incompatible you can just walk out. Also, marriage makes people complacent. If you live together you might try harder.

Denise believes living together is a responsible stage in making a stable marriage later. She thinks it is important to know if you are sexually compatible and if you can put up with each other's peculiar habits.

Phil is convinced that living together is a great option. You are free to love and go as you choose, without any ties or responsibilities. He thinks Ray is crazy.

General discussion

What do you think of the reasons John, Jenny, Denise and Phil gave for not getting married?
What do you think of Andrea and Ray's reasons for getting married?
Why do you think Jenny believes that marriage makes people complacent and if they lived together they might try harder?
Is sexual compatibility instantaneous, or does it develop in the security of a committed relationship, as a couple learn more about their partner's needs and fears, and what they enjoy and what they do not?

If you live with someone are there any 'ties and responsibilities'? If not, why not? If there are, what are they?

90 per cent of women in our society will marry at some stage in their lives, and 86 per cent of men. Why do you think marriage is so popular?

Research shows that couples who live together before marriage have a higher divorce rate than those who do not. Can you think of any reasons why this should happen?

CASE STUDY: SALLY AND ALAN

Sally and Alan visit a marriage counsellor. They have been married for ten years and have a son and a daughter. Tom is eight and Tessa is five-and-a-half. They had married in church and everything was fine for the first six years. Then things started to go wrong. Alan's business ran into difficulties and money was very tight. Sally's adored father died and her relationship with her mother, which was never very good, had got worse. Sally thought she was always comparing her children unfavourably with her sisters'. Alan said this was nonsense and just proved how paranoid Sally had become. He accused her of changing from a loving wife and daughter into an over-protective and possessive mother. 'She even tries to turn the children against me.' Sally denies this strongly and acknowledges that Alan is a good father. Nevertheless, she has decided that she can't go on. She wants to leave Alan and take the children with her. She has a small sum of money that her father has left her and wants to be independent. 'I can't help it', she says, 'I don't love him any more and there is nothing that I can do about it.'

How is Sally feeling?

How is Alan feeling?

How do you think Sally's mother is feeling?

How do you think Tom and Tessa are being affected by the situation?

Sally's 'adored father' had died during the past four years. What support would she have needed from Alan to help her through her grief?

Alan's business has been affected badly during the past four years. What support did he need from Sally to help him cope with the situation?

When Sally says 'I don't love him any more and there is nothing I can do about it' what does she mean? Do people decide to stop loving each other or does it happen against their will?

The Children Act 1989 states that although parents may be divorced, they are both equally responsible for the children. How will this affect Sally's determination to bring up the children independently of Alan?

Is this marriage bound to fail or is there anything the counsellor can do to help the couple save the relationship?

REFLECTION EXERCISE

(Personal to the individual)

CAN WE RECOGNIZE TRUE LOVE?

When I think about my relationship with my parents I _____

When I think about my relationship with my friends I _____

When I think about my relationship with God I _____

Loving somebody means _____

Not loving means _____

People who love me _____

When I think of the people I love I _____

A happy family is _____

I know —— loves me because _____

I felt unloved when _____

I felt loved when _____

For me, marriage means _____

When I think of intimacy I _____

When I think of commitment I _____

What I hope to teach my children about love is _____

I could become a more loving person by _____

The most important person in my life at the moment is _____

SEVEN GUIDELINES FOR MORALLY LOVING BEHAVIOUR

A group of American Christian theologians suggested seven guidelines for morally loving behaviour. A loving relationship will be:

Self-liberating
Other-enriching
Honest
Faithful
Socially responsible
Life-serving
Joyous

LOVE IS ——

Sample:

Love is ——
Intimate
Natural
Caring
Open
a **M**ust
Patient
Respectful
Equal
Honest
Exquisite
Never easy
Sharing
Innovative
Building
Lasting
Exciting
INCOMPREHENSIBLE

(Composed by a group on an Arundel and Brighton Youth Weekend.)

Individually or small groups
Complete the unfinished sentence in your own words:

Love is _____

PINCH/CRUNCH MODEL

Beginning a relationship

Two people meet. They find each other interesting and begin to exchange information about themselves, asking questions, exploring, offering bits of their personal stories to each other. They have begun a relationship.

As well as sharing their personal stories, thoughts, feelings and opinions with each other, they begin to do things together, spending time together in a common experience. As their relationship develops, so too do the expectations they may have of each other, e.g. they expect the other to keep Saturday evenings free so that they can be together. Spoken as well as unspoken commitments, both large and small, may be offered and expected.

Ups and downs

If the relationship continues to be satisfying as they meet each other's expectations, they may develop a closer relationship. They clarify regular arrangements and roles and thus deepen their commitment to each other.

When a couple are agreed about their roles and have a degree of commitment, their relationship enters a period when everything seems stable. A sense of equilibrium prevails.

Stability in a relationship, however, seldom lasts long. Inevitably there comes a *pinch*. A pinch is a feeling of dissatisfaction, a 'niggle' or negative feeling usually to do with unfulfilled expectations. Dismay at being let down, hurt when some 'promise' is not kept, a perceived breach of confidence, these and other similar mismatches between what they expected and what actually happened are typical pinches in any relationship.

Restoring stability

A pinch can be dealt with in three ways:

1   Ignore it. Many people do this at first, hoping the negative feelings will go away. Why rock the boat? We've been getting on so well. Sometimes this works; more often, it goes away only to return reinforced when the next pinch is felt. Now there are two pinches to deal with . . .

2   Deal with it indirectly. Hint at your hurt feelings. Make a 'joke' of it. Kiss and make up without really talking about it. Why spoil things by making a mountain out of a molehill?

3   Talk it out. Share your feelings. Renegotiate your expectations.

Adapted from John J. Sherwood and John J. Scherer, *The Dating Mating Game: How to Play Without Losing* (Purdue University, 1974). Multiple copies of this page may be made by the purchasing organization only.

Failure to restore stability

Pinches are uncomfortable but they are opportunities for growth. Ways of coping that avoid confronting the problem, e.g. ignoring it, trying to solve the problem alone, 'offering things up' will not work in the long run. The quality of the relationship will ultimately be weakened unless we are prepared to share our negative as well as positive feelings. Each unresolved pinch will create a bigger communication gap within the relationship, making the next pinch harder to deal with and producing a bigger and bigger stack of unfinished business.

Crunch points

Where pinches are not dealt with effectively, they often lead to a *crunch* point. A crunch is an intolerable situation where both partners know there is something seriously wrong. The relationship is in crisis. Invariably, they are communicating badly and may be hurting each other more and more. Trust and respect for each other may be diminishing rapidly. Love seems very far away.

Unsuccessful ways out of a crunch

1 Forget the past and start again. Unfortunately, mere resolutions are not the answer and lead to new pinches and crunches.

2 Stay together for the sake of appearances. The relationship is psychologically dead. All that is left is cold war and co-existence.

3 The big bust-up, which is the nearest thing to a pitched battle. The couple get locked into a circular argument and cannot break out of it, e.g. He nags because she drinks. She drinks because he nags. The defend–attack spiral of mutual recrimination can continue for years.

4 The fourth and sometimes successful way is to renegotiate under stress. The stress is not helpful, but building a new relationship on stronger foundations is possible if the will to do so exists on both sides. This is the time when outside help is necessary and the couple need to consult a professional counsellor.

Pinches and crunches, then, are both choice points. Each time we sort out a pinch and renegotiate our expectations of each other we grow closer and strengthen the relationship. Each time we leave pinches unsolved we move that much nearer to a crunch!

Adapted from John J. Sherwood and John J. Scherer, *The Dating Mating Game: How to Play Without Losing* (Purdue University, 1974). Multiple copies of this page may be made by the purchasing organization only.

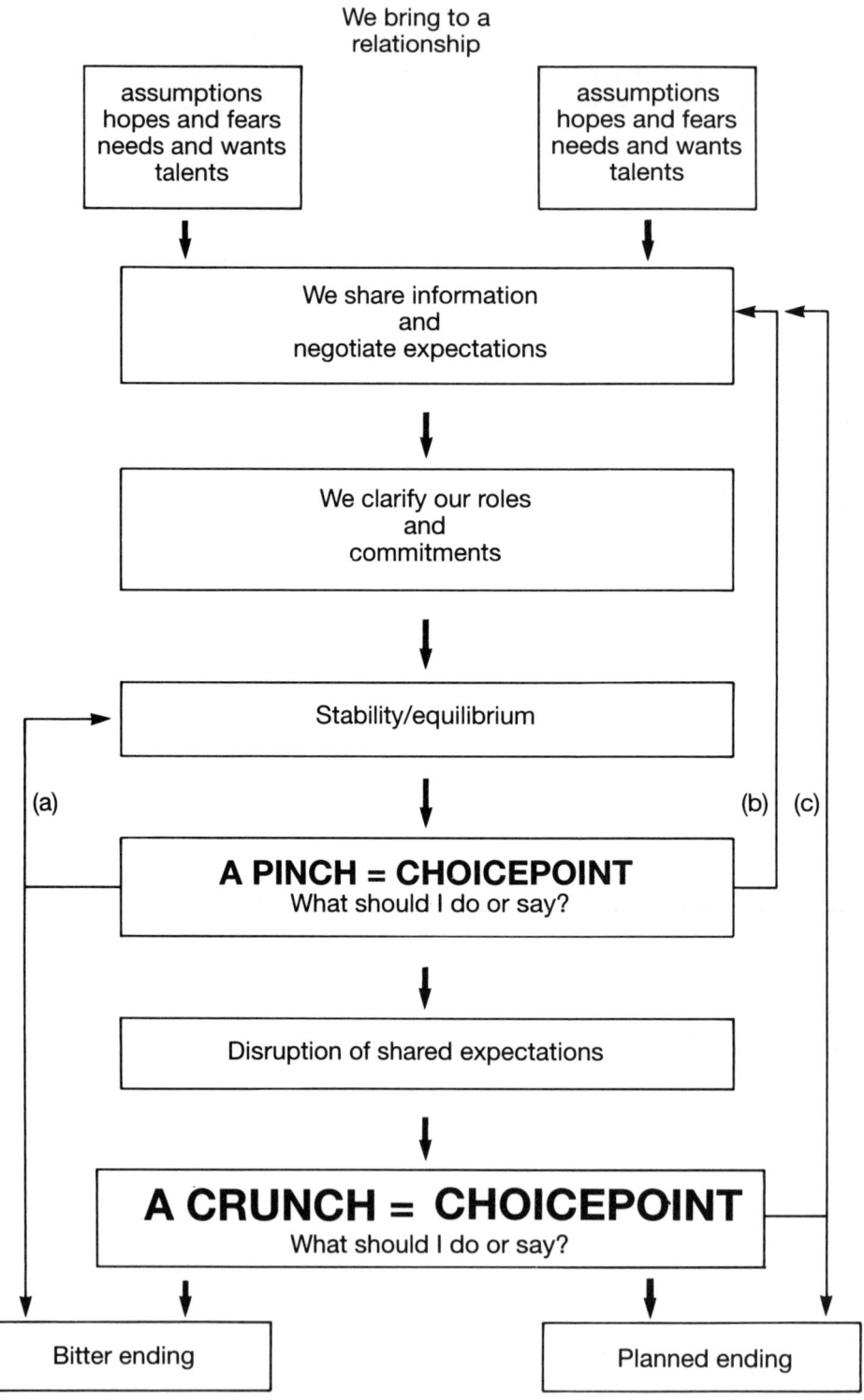

(a) ignore it (b) renegotiate it (c) renegotiate it under stress

HOW TO AVOID THE DEFEND/ ATTACK SPIRAL

1   Count to ten before responding, taking a couple of deep breaths while doing so.

2   First acknowledge the feeling that is being presented to you and the other person's reason for feeling it, e.g. 'I realize you are annoyed because I am late again'.

3   Offer your feelings in response, including saying sorry if you feel sorry. If you don't feel sorry, don't say so unless it seems courteous to do so.

4   Offer an explanation if this is needed or demanded. Be prepared for it to be rejected if the other person is still angry or experiencing some other strong emotion. *Repeat yourself if necessary.*

In pairs

Take it in turns to identify a situation which you would find difficult to manage. Write down an example of the aggressive remarks that might be used to you so that your partner can say them to you with the appropriate level of feeling! In response, practise your drill and discuss with your partner the effect it would have. If necessary, change the script and try again.

ASSERTIVENESS SELF-ASSESSMENT QUESTIONNAIRE

Behaviour	People					
Expressing positive feelings	Friends of the same sex	Friends of the opposite sex	Intimates, e.g. boy-friend, girl-friend	Parents, aunts, uncles	Brothers or sisters	Teachers and other authority figures
Give compliments						
Receive compliments						
Ask for things: help, favours, etc.						
Express liking						
Start and maintain conversations						
Self-affirmation						
Stand up for your rights						
Refuse requests						
Express opinions including disagreement						
Expressing negative feelings						
Express annoyance, displeasure, hurt						
Express justified anger						

Use ticks and crosses to find out where you find it most difficult to speak assertively.
Alternatively, use a simple code to indicate degrees of difficulty,
e.g. VE = very easy, QE = quite easy, D = difficult, I = impossible.

Adapted from Colleen Kelly, *Assertion Training: A Facilitator's Guide* (University Associates, 1979). Multiple copies of this page may be made by the purchasing organization only.